PRAISE FOR LIKE A ROARING LION

"Rob's experiences with the Lord will challenge you to be bold and confident in your prayers and faith. Through the examples, he shares you can't deny the power in the name of Jesus. He wonderfully lays out how we should react if for some reason God chooses not to heal or answer the prayers we are praying. These true-life stories will encourage you to go deeper with God and to trust in Him for any and all situations you are going through."

—Emily Sarmiento, director of Orlando House of Prayer

"This was not just a journey to understand prayer, but a quest to make one's relationship with God their own. In this beautiful book, you see Rob actually leaning into God as he struggled. He walked away from church for a while and from some of the things he'd been taught. But he didn't really walk away from God… He wouldn't let him!"

—Kay Harms, social media influencer, author, and blogger

"Like a Roaring Lion is a story of genuine faith that points to Jesus. Rob is honest about his doubts and deep struggles with his faith. I could relate to his feelings of despair, wondering how I could be a new creation, a true believer, and feel as I did. The God-ordained encounters

Rob shares are nothing short of incredible, as is the peaceful faith he continues to walk in today. It is a wonderful read. Don't miss the opportunity to share his journey."

—Chrissy Rowden, influencer and marketing creative

LIKE A ROARING LION

ONE MAN'S JOURNEY INTO SPIRITUAL WARFARE

ROBERT FILOGOMO

Like a Roaring Lion
Copyright © 2022 by Robert Filogomo

All rights reserved. No part of this book may be reproduced in any form or by any means—whether electronic, digital, mechanical, or otherwise—without permission in writing from the publisher, except by a reviewer, who may quote brief passages in a review.

Unless otherwise noted, all Scripture verses are from the Holy Bible, New International Version®, NIV® Copyright ©1973, 1978, 1984, 2011 by Biblica, Inc.® Used by permission. All rights reserved worldwide. Scripture texts, prefaces, introductions, footnotes and cross references used in this work marked NABRE are taken from the New American Bible, revised edition © 2010, 1991, 1986, 1970 Confraternity of Christian Doctrine, Inc., Washington, DC All Rights Reserved. No part of this work may be reproduced or transmitted in any form or by any means, electronic or mechanical, including photocopying, recording, or by any information storage and retrieval system, without permission in writing from the copyright owner.

The views and opinions expressed in this book are those of the author and do not necessarily reflect the official policy or position of Illumify Media Global.

Published by
Illumify Media Global
www.IllumifyMedia.com
"*Let's bring your book to life!*"

Library of Congress Control Number:

Paperback ISBN: 978-1-955043-63-2

Typeset by Art Innovations (http://artinnovations.in/)
Cover design by Debbie Lewis

Printed in the United States of America

*To all my family and friends who are no longer here.
Gone too soon but no more tears, no more pain.
Looking towards our joyful reunion.*

CONTENTS

Preface	xiii
Introduction	xvii
1. "You did what?"	1
2. God Kept Showing Up	3
3. New York Bound	15
4. A Day in Hell's Kitchen	29
5. The Harlem Voodoo Building	39
6. Tarot Readers and Supernatural Bats	47
7. The House Guest from Hell	57
8. Rock and Roll, the Occult, and Josh's Story	69
9. The Intervention	79
10. The Roar of the Lion	87
11. I Want to Believe	91
12. The Camping Trip Like No Other	97
13. The Camping Trip Strangers	103
14. My Dying Friend Joe	111
Epilogue	119
About the Author	123

"Be alert and of sober mind. Your enemy the devil prowls around like a roaring lion looking for someone to devour."
(1 Peter 5:8)

PREFACE

I've had the relentless desire to tell my story about supernatural events that I have experienced. Things most people would describe as unbelievable!

What has stopped me from sharing my experiences all these years?

For starters, professionally I'm a math guy and not a writer by trade, so it felt like a daunting task. I also knew the stories would give an intimate glimpse into my personal life and beliefs. Did I really want to open this portion of my private self for public viewing? The thought filled me with fear. I was afraid of ridicule and failure.

But something else unnerved me even more: that I was not worthy to proclaim my love for God publicly.

Which, of course, led to procrastination.

I also wanted to make sure I got all the details of these amazing events written down accurately. Quite frankly, some of the incidentals about people I met along the way have gotten fuzzy with the passage of years. I may not remember if someone had a beard or what their first name really was—but the supernatural interventions that I experienced impacted me in such a way that I remember them as vividly as if they happened yesterday.

I have relied on my memory to recreate conversations and timelines, and I have changed the names of people in my stories to respect their privacy.

I could not have done this without the support of my beautiful, talented, and dedicated wife, Jodie. She pushed me out of my procrastination and my comfort zone multiple times yet without giving up on me. We are truly soulmates, and she is the love of my life.

This book would not be possible without the talent and support of my writing coach, Karen Bouchard. Her assistance, guidance, and encouragement helped make my experiences and thoughts come alive on paper.

And a big Thank you to Geoffrey Stone, editorial director, Illumify Media Global for his guidance with the nuances of copyediting which made the book better.

Finally, I want to acknowledge Michael Klassen, president of Illumify Media Global, and all the incredibly talented people on the Illumify team.

What are my intentions for writing this book? I certainly don't want to debate theology. So, what do I want? I want to:

- stir your faith in God,
- give you hope,

- sound the alarm that fierce battles are raging between good and evil,
- shout to the world that God is *not* dead, and
- yes, convince you that evil exists.

What you are about to read is not only true, but it can also change your life.

It did mine.

INTRODUCTION

I turned my back on everything I believed about God. Well, almost everything.

And I'm not alone. I've met many people who have turned their backs on what they believed. Some embrace the idea that you can make your own reality by consistently speaking to the universe to send blessings into your life. Most equate the universe with God. Some conclude that evil is a mindset, and the devil doesn't really exist. But this nonexistent devil was killing my friends and squeezing the life out of me with fear.

During many years of helping the homeless on the streets of Denver, Boulder, New York City, and Paris, France, I've had numerous encounters with the darkness of evil. I've lost friends; some died because of bad advice and church teachings. But I've also had many instances where God protected me from Satan.

In the following pages, I share intimate glimpses into my personal life and describe my astonishing experiences.

I demonstrate how I worked through doubts and questions.

I disclose which prayers work for me and which do not.

I reveal the scars obtained while in battle with evil.

I hide nothing, including my own faith crisis, anger towards God, and what it took to bring about my reconciliation with Him.

No matter what we believe, we all make choices to be on the side of good or on the side of evil. And no matter if you see it or believe it, God does move in the here and now. This is not a theological treatise nor a promotion of one type of church over another. It is an honest glimpse of my challenges, my victories, and my faith throughout my life.

Do you believe God exists? Do you believe Satan exits?

Read on before making up your mind.

1

"YOU DID WHAT?"

"YOU DID WHAT?" I exclaimed.

"I signed you up to spend the summer with Teen Challenge in New York City working with teenaged drug addicts," my friend James repeated and then added, "I already put down a deposit for you to go."

It was 1984, a perfect autumn day with the crisp blue air and the warm Colorado sun warming our souls. James and I were sitting with a few other friends on a deck, attending a low-key bachelor party for one of our mutual buddies.

"In fact," he said, looking at our friend Don, "I signed you up too."

Don laughed. "That's great, but where am I supposed to get the money to do something like that?"

"I've got the same question," I added with a grin.

"You have a few weeks to think about if you want to do it or not," James said. "But I think it is right up your alley."

I had met James on the streets of Boulder three or four years earlier when we were both volunteering with the homeless. James was the manager of a youth coffeehouse on Pearl Street where I'd been singing and talking to people about Jesus. James and I would often get together at Perkins after we finished for the evening for great theological discussions. These were some of the best times of my life.

A breeze blew across the deck. I looked at James and Don.

James added, "Besides, I've been praying, and I really think this is something God wants for you. But you need to pray about it too and see what He tells you."

I didn't need to pray about it. From the instant James had made the surprising announcement, God had confirmed in my heart that He had been leading me to this moment for some time.

"I'm in," I said.

"Me too," added Don. "I was feeling something like this would present itself. Count me in as well."

I wasn't a stranger to God showing up in my life. He had been part of my life as long as I could remember.

Maybe it had something to do with the prayer of a frantic mother, desperate to save the life of her two-year-old son.

2

GOD KEPT SHOWING UP

"HE'S BURNING UP!" my mom told my aunt and grandmother over the phone. I was two and had been feverish for days. "We're doing everything the doctors tell us, but the fever won't let him go."

The two women rallied the entire family to pray. My grandmother prayed faithfully on her rosary beads every day. A few days later, out of exhaustion and desperation, my mom cried out to God: "I promise I will raise him to love You if You make him better!"

The fever broke. Within a few days, I had completely recovered. God had answered Mom's prayer, and she never let me forget it!

"You were so hot when I put ointment on your little body to cool you down, the ointment would bubble!" she would say.

As a teenager, I would roll my eyes and laugh. "I don't think a person can get that hot."

But I always wondered.

Was it just a coincidence? Did my mom's prayer just happen to coincide with the timing of me getting well?

Deep down inside, I knew. My healing when I was two was the beginning of God's inventions in my life.

By the age of three, I was studying music, compliments of my uncle. After seeing a kid playing the vibraphone on the Micky Mouse Club, his goal for me was to play the vibes. When I turned four, he bought me a full-size vibraphone, which I loved and practiced playing every day.

"I've noticed Robby squinting," Mr. Del, my music teacher, said to my uncle. "He is struggling with reading the sheet music."

"Yes," my uncle agreed. "He squints his eyes and leans forward when practicing."

Mr. Del told my parents, who scheduled me an eye exam right away.

"Robby needs reading glasses," the eye doctor announced.

"He's only four years old!" my mom protested loudly.

"He has a slight stigmatism and is nearsighted," the doctor explained. "This is why it is hard for him to read the notes on the sheet music."

Within a week, I had glasses.

"Wow!" I exclaimed, "my glasses really help me see the sheet music, and I love my cowboy embossed eyeglass case. Thanks, Mom."

Two years later, I began attending first grade at a Catholic school in our town. I remember waiting for the school bus on my front stoop, dressed in my little gray uniform slacks, my freshly pressed white uniform shirt, and my green clip-on tie.

A few weeks into the school year, during one of our religious education hours, Sister Mary Carmel told us the story of Jesus and what he did for us. I remember being mesmerized with the way she told the story. Her voice and intonations transported us back in time. She made us feel like we were right there in the time of Jesus. The gentleness in her voice as she described the love that motivated Jesus to sacrifice His life for us was so moving it brought me to tears.

That's when I said to myself, "I want Jesus as my friend and to save me."

Immediately, I felt a warm light enter my stomach, and I started to cry.

"What is wrong?" Sister Carmel asked.

"I felt very emotional as you were telling us the story of Jesus," I replied with a sniffle. "And when you told us how He rose from the dead, I asked Him to love me. Then!" I said excitedly, "I felt a warmth inside me. It felt so warm, like a blanket wrapped around me after a day playing in the snow."

All she could do was hug me.

I arrived home later that afternoon. After some cookies and milk, it was time to practice my vibes. I put my glasses on, set up the sheet music on the music stand, and began my music exercises. I did my scales, arpeggios, and mallet exercises. Then it was time to work on the piece of music I was learning for that week.

I played the familiar first few bars of music, but when

I reached the parts I was unfamiliar with, I noticed I couldn't see the notes clearly.

"Mom, I think I am having trouble seeing again," I called to my mom.

Another trip to the eye doctor revealed something startling! My eyes had suddenly corrected themselves. One day I had needed those glasses. The next day my eyes had been healed. And the only thing that had happened out of the ordinary between those two days was that I'd had an encounter with Jesus.

God continued showing up in my life. Even when I lost touch with my faith and found myself going down some dangerous paths, He never let go of me.

After attending Catholic school for six years, I transferred to a public junior high school. I quickly found out that public school was much different than Catholic school.

I felt lost.

"Mr. Filogomo, what did you do over the summer break?" my teacher asked. It was my first day. I stood up to answer her question, as any good Catholic schoolboy would do. The class erupted into laughter.

"Who stands up to answer a question?" I heard one kid say loudly.

"Mr. Filogomo, in the future you do not need to stand when answering questions in this school," the teacher said kindly.

"I played lots of baseball." I said, embarrassed, and quickly sat down.

I hated that none of my friends were in any of my classes. I abhorred combination lockers. I detested that the school felt like a maze to me. Trying to fit in, I fell in with the drug crowd. I was no longer ignored when walking down the hall. Kids greeted me like their longtime friend. I felt included, I felt like a somebody.

Unfortunately, I dragged my childhood friends from my neighborhood into this lifestyle, and we all became potheads. I barely held onto my faith, but I never denied Jesus when asked about Him. And while I continued to pray every day, my conscience slowly became calloused, making prayer harder and harder.

But the Lord was always there. He protected me during a group fight, allowing me to escape unharmed. And He frequently allowed me to avoid getting arrested.

I wasted so much time. I had so much regret.

Then I met a girl.

After a few months of dating, my high school sweetheart questioned my druggie lifestyle. Laurie persuasively pointed out the downfalls of using drugs. Honestly, I was so tired of being a pothead I was looking for any excuse to give it up.

As Laurie got to know me better, she encouraged me to pursue my love of music. I began reengaging in writing songs and performing in coffeehouses. I was having fun. With a clear head and Laurie by my side, I pushed back on the peer pressure and refused the offers of pot and temptations of other destructive habits.

When Laurie suggested we stop seeing each other since we were heading to different colleges in the fall, I returned to pot and alcohol to numb the heartache but quickly realized I no longer enjoyed the hazy feeling.

Arriving at college, it was easy to start partying

again. But my roommate, who loved Jesus, reminded me what living a godly life looked like—in actions not just words.

God hadn't forgotten me. He had protected me. He had intervened in my life—again!

He was inviting me to go deeper in relationship with him, and I said yes with all my heart.

My sophomore and junior years of college at the University of Colorado Boulder I became involved with a few on-campus Christian youth ministries. The groups of kids in these ministries were from all different flavors of Christianity: Catholics, Baptists, Lutheran, Presbyterian, and something I had never heard of, nondenominational and Charismatic. Some of us kids in the group became friends.

One day one of the girls said, "Hey, Rob, what if we met weekly to pray for different things and people's needs? We could pray healing prayers for friends or family."

"We could pray for friends with broken or struggling relationships," someone else added.

And everyone agreed that we could pray for guidance in our own lives.

"That sounds like a great idea," I answered excitedly. "We can use my dorm room as a meeting place."

Our prayer group grew, and that's where I met my friend Angie.

She and her roommate, Lena, would also visit our church occasionally. It was at this church where I first met my friend Don. My initial impression was not favorable. He came across as a typical wise guy city boy.

"Hey, Don." I said as we both walked into Sunday services. "It's nice to see you here this morning."

"Hi, Rob, do you mind if I catch a seat with you?" Don asked a tad nervously.

"No problem, I'm sitting over there on the left."

As I interacted with Don, I noticed God's transformation taking place in his life.

He became a regular at all the church services, and we began hanging out together. We engaged in many conversations about faith, and to my surprise we became friends. God changed the fast-talking city boy into a kindhearted person.

I cherished my friends, my clear mind, and my resurrected relationship with Jesus.

During college I was fortunate to go home for the holidays every year. That time of year has always been a wonderful time at my house. As an Italian American Roman Catholic family, we would always celebrate Christmas Eve with the Feast of Seven Fishes. This celebration always included a spectacular Italian feast with a variety of seafood dishes that my mom prepared masterfully.

We enjoyed stuffed lobster tails with crabmeat; fillet of flounder cutlets; steamed clams, shrimp, and mussels in tomato sauce; and baccala which is a salted cod fish that Mom would cook for hours in tomato sauce. And that was just the seafood!

Mom also served lasagna and various vegetable dishes such as string beans in olive oil; broccoli rabe with garlic, olive oil and Italian spices; and Italian salad—not to mention her incredibly addictive chicken cutlets.

She also made the best calamari I have ever tasted. Her calamari were so unlike the fried rubber bands that is so common in some restaurants. In fact, they weren't fried at all. I remember her spending hours cleaning the squid, then seasoning it to perfection. It was always so tender. I didn't think she could prepare it any better until the year she served the calamari in a thick Italian marinara sauce over spaghetti. Wow! I would eat an entire loaf of bread just sopping up the sauce.

When my dad was alive, he would order the seafood for this feast at the local seafood market a month ahead of time. The seafood was always fresh and top quality. Typically, about twenty of us gathered for dinner, but my mom had enough food to feed a hundred, no exaggeration.

My mom masterfully pulled together this amazing experience year in and year out. What a great mom!

Later in the evening, we would open presents and then attend midnight mass at our neighborhood church. Afterward, my mom, brothers, and I would stay up late and talk, laugh, play games, and solve the world's problems.

I'll never forget the Christmas when something happened that impacted my faith for years to come. Arriving home after mass, we all stayed up playing Bible Trivia Pursuit until the early hours of the morning. After the last game, everyone went to bed except for one of my brothers and me. We stayed seated around the kitchen table and chatted.

During the Bible game some interesting theological questions about healing had come up. As we discussed them, my brother told me about a friend of his who was dealing with cancer and wanted to know my thoughts about healing for today.

"I believe God does heal in this day and age," I answered.

"Always?"

I shook my head. "I wish. We both know that sometimes He doesn't. But," I added, "everything we do should always be bathed in prayer. We can try to understand God's will in each situation but there are forces and ancient powers, and we are not aware how they work, or what and who they are."

He nodded.

"Let's pray for your friend," I offered.

"Cool. But hold on a second because I want to get my rosary beads, the ones Diana gave me from her trip to Medjugorje."

I knew of Medjugorje. It was a small hamlet in Bosnia-Herzegovina where, in the early '80s, six children began having daily conversations with the Blessed Virgin Mary.

He returned with his rosary, and we started to pray.

Suddenly he lifted his hands to the ceiling in worship, raising the rosary beads with his hands. To my utter amazement his rosary beads started to glow. He opened his eyes and saw them glowing as well. We both rubbed our eyes and looked again.

Yes, his beads were still glowing, a bright yellow, like polished gold in sunlight!

As we were observing this phenomenon, I couldn't help but start to sing praise songs to God. My brother also started singing praises, and the more we sang, the brighter the beads glowed.

We both marveled.

"This is incredible!" I gasped.

Then, overcome with emotion, we both started to laugh hysterically and continued praising God. With all the commotion we were making, we must have awakened the entire household.

Mom showed up in the kitchen and asked, "What's going on?"

My other brothers stumbling down the stairs right behind her, each asking the same question.

Just as fast as the beads had started to glow, they stopped.

My brother and I looked at the beads. We were at a loss for how to even start to explain what had happened. Plus, we couldn't stop laughing! The joy of the Lord continued bubbling out of us. In fact, the more we tried to explain, the more we laughed. It must have been contagious because then my mom started to laugh uncontrollably as did my other brothers. There we all were, in my mom's tiny little kitchen, laughing hysterically until our sides hurt.

When we managed to calm down enough for my brother and me to describe what had just happened, everyone was flabbergasted. My brother and I just marveled at what we just experienced.

Sometimes things happen when you least expect it.

One of the most fearful calls I have ever made was to

my mom. "I am so disappointed," my mom answered when I told her my plans. "You just quit your senior year of collage to go save the world?" she asked. "Can't you save the world and finish college at the same time?"

But I couldn't.

Although I had some amazing experiences and eventually obtained my master's of science degree, looking back I feel dropping out of college was one of the worst decisions I ever made. But God continued to move in my life anyway.

One day my paster called. "Hey, Rob, would you and your friends consider working with me and some of the local churches on Saturday mornings?" he asked. "I need help bringing food and clothing to the homeless."

"Don't you kids have anything better to do with your time then to pass out sandwiches?" a homeless lady screeched as tears filled her eyes.

Another time a local pastor we knew contacted me. "Hi, Rob, would you and your friends like to help the Denver Rescue Mission once in a while with their daily church service?"

Standing up front at the Rescue Mission I introduce our group.

"Hi, we are from local churches here in Denver," I said. "We are here to sing praise songs to Jesus, and I hope you all join in."

"Hey, you sound like dying geese," one heckler yelled before we even started to sing. Others joined in ridiculing us. It was getting somewhat loud and uncomfortable. But we soldiered on and started to sing praise and worship songs to Jesus.

One big guy who had a weathered face from what I imagine were years of hard living came up to us. Staring me in the face, I could smell his stale breath. Then he turned and yelled, "Quiet!" motioning to the other rabble rousers.

As we continued to sing, one by one we could hear from the crowd, "Jesus loves me this I know" and then "I love you Lord and I lift my voice." They joined in singing all the songs we were playing. We could not hold back our tears!

Afterward, as we were packing up to leave, broken men of all shapes and sizes would look around to make sure no one was looking and came up to us with their broken smiles and would muster up a simple, "thank you."

I was hooked. My heart was pulling me in the direction of doing what I thought were the basics of helping people. The thought of children and families not knowing where their next meal was coming from or where they were going to spend the night was a growing problem. It just broke my heart.

3

NEW YORK BOUND

AFTER JAMES TOLD me he had signed me and Don up to go to New York—and I felt confirmation from the Holy Spirit that this is what He wanted me to do—I quickly realized I did not have money to make the trip. I was working in a warehouse and delivering furniture to make ends meet. I prayed that the funds would present themselves. I didn't know How as I had little time to pick up a third job since I stayed busy working on the streets of Boulder and Denver helping with the homeless people. Amazingly, somehow both Don and I managed to leap over all the hurdles—emotional and financial—that stood in our way.

God had made it possible for us to go on this incredible trip!

Our plan was to stay with my mom for the summer while we ministered on the streets. Naturally, my mom was ecstatic. From her house in Yorktown Heights, we could take a forty-five-minute train ride into the city.

One of the big perks of staying with Mom—besides saving money and seeing family—was the chance that she would make her famous eggplant parmesan sandwiches for us to take for our lunches.

A few days before I left for my adventure in New York City the phone rang.

"Oh, hi, Mom," I said. "I am excited to see you in a few days."

"Hi, honey," mom said, "I have bad news. Grandma just had a slight stroke and is in the hospital."

I immediately started making calls, asking friends, colleagues, and even acquaintances to please pray for my grandma. Now there are different thoughts on the physical healing power of God.

My friend Art believed that God doesn't miraculously heal people anymore. When I asked him to pray for my grandmother, he said, "Sure, Rob. I will pray that God comforts you and your family in this time of need."

I called another friend, Arlean. She seemed to believe that it might not be God's will to heal. "Sure Rob," she said and launched into a prayer right then: "God, we know you can do miracles. Please comfort and teach Rob's family what you want them to learn." She ended her prayer with the words, "Your will be done in Jesus' name, Amen."

I had questions. People had such different views on healing.

The big day finally arrived. I backed my Toyota pickup out of the driveway and aimed it toward the freeway. We were going to New York City!

It was a beautiful, clear summer of 1985 morning in

Boulder. There was an unusual, beautiful orange glow reflecting off the mountains from the morning sunrise. Don and I took this as a particularly good sign that our decision to go the New York City was the right decision.

I admitted to Don, "One month ago, I never would have imagined that in four shorts weeks we would be on our way to minister on some of the most dangerous streets in New York City. It still amazes me," I added, "how—after James signed us up in the Teen Challenge summer program—our circumstances and planning just fell into place. I am still humbled that James offered to pay for all the signup fees for both of us."

We drove straight through from Boulder Colorado to Yorktown Heights, New York. It took us a little over thirty-five hours. One of us would sometimes sleep in the back of my pickup while the other drove. Actually, it was a great system, but I would never in a million years drive like that again.

On the drive, I spent time thinking about my grandma. I had rallied many friends to pray for her, even though their thoughts on healing were diverse.

Was it possible? Could God heal her?

I was very close to Grandma. When I was growing up, my Aunt Mary and Uncle Sal were like my second parents. My house was at the bottom of the hill in our New York suburbia housing development. Aunt Mary's house was about ten houses up the street. Grandma lived with my aunt and uncle.

Grandma would say in her broken English, "Your parents and Aunt Mary and Uncle Sal are out, so you are staying the night."

"Oh boy!" I would respond. "Are we going to watch the *Lawrence Welk Show*?"

I have great memories of watching the *Lawrence Welk Show* with Grandma. It was her favorite TV show.

If I were sick and had to stay home from school, I would stay with Grandma at Aunt Mary's house during the day.

"Grandma, my stomach hurts," I would whine.

"I will make for you my special bay leaf tea with a hint of sugar," she would assure me. This concoction would settle my stomach almost immediately.

One summer, she gazed at her garden and said, "Robby, will you look at my beautiful tomatoes, string beans, Italian peppers, and zucchini!" She added, "You can grow your own little garden if you want."

"I would love to grow stuff!" I responded with excitement.

When I was nine, my grandma and I made a special spot for me in her garden.

"Robby, why don't you start with green beans," she suggested.

"Great!" I yelled, "I love string beans!"

"Look grandma," I said one day, "the rabbits seem to only like *your* string beans." They had eaten almost her entire crop, but they hadn't touched even one plant of mine.

Grandma, in her broken English, marveled. "Why the rabbits only like my string beans and not yours?"

We never figured that one out. But another day, we caught an unusual thief, one who had been stealing her tomatoes for some time.

"Grandma, look!" I yelled. "It's the tomato thief!"

We ran to the tomato section just as Grandma's little dog, Ripper, a gray mini version of a long-haired husky, jumped over the garden fence with a tomato in his mouth.

Grandma chased Ripper and yelled at him in Italian to drop the tomato while I fell on the ground laughing hysterically.

I love those memories. My grandma was such a wonderful woman.

I looked over at Don in the passenger seat of the Toyota pickup. He was fast asleep. With a long road before us, I let my mind continue to wander. This time I thought about all the things I had been learning and hearing about healing.

Art had prayed more for comfort than healing. Arlean had prayed as though God might not heal.

But I knew plenty of people who took a very different approach. In fact, most everyone at my church believed that no one needed to be sick, that everyone could be healed by God. That certainly was an appealing thought. In fact, I knew some people who believed that if you had strong enough faith and lived a sinless life, but who can do this? (Romans 3:10) you wouldn't die at all —just be taken away when your time came to leave this earth.

One pastor said, "If you're sick, it's because of some sin in your life. Get the sin out of your life to receive your healing." Another pastor asked, "Why didn't you get healed? I will tell you why. It is because you did not have enough faith." On TV a pastor yelled, "If you have faith, stop taking your medicine. And stop sinning. Believe what the Bibles says."

I loved the idea of not being sick, but the more I heard, the more I felt something was wrong with these ideas.

Or was it me? Did I just not have enough faith?

As I drove, I reflected on an experience I'd had recently when a friend of mine was diagnosed with breast cancer. "Rob," Gwen had told me, her eyes filled with anticipation and faith, "I have decided not to do any of the treatments recommended by my doctor. My sin is washed away, and I have faith in what the Bible tells me."

"I will fast and pray for your healing," I had assured her. Deep inside I'd thought she should accept the treatments, but I'd been afraid to tell her.

A few weeks later, Gwen's husband called. She had landed in the hospital.

"Can I visit her?" I'd asked.

"Rob, come down in a few days. She is starting cancer treatment immediately. It's quite urgent."

Within a matter of weeks, she was gone.

She hadn't been the first member of our church to die under similar circumstances. After her funeral I remember processing her death with a friend of ours. "I am concerned we are losing great friends," I'd told him. "I know they had faith, but they are dying anyway."

"Who knows?" my friend had chimed in. "Maybe they would have died anyway even with medical treatment. But we will never know."

"For a long time now, I've been feeling that something is not right with this notion of not taking medicine."

My friend had nodded. "Maybe it's like we are testing God."

"Exactly!" I'd agreed. "Like we are daring Him to heal us. Or trying to convince Him that we have this incredible faith that gives us the right to demand Him to heal us."

"I heard someone say that!" my friend had blurted out. "I head one of the big faith guys say that because of the covenant God made with us, we should demand He heal us. And if He doesn't heal us, we should call Him a liar."

"Wow!" I shuddered. "Where is the reverence? Where is the respect?"

My friend had nodded somberly. "I always thought God allowed men and women of science to discover and invent medicines and procedures to help heal our bodies," he said. "My thoughts have always been, stay on your medicines but think positively and pray, too."

"I know," I'd chimed in again, "Studies are showing that positive thinking, laughter, and prayer helps with the healing process. Let us not throw the baby out with the bath water."

My friend had agreed.

These memories and others mingled in my mind as I drove. We serve a God of power and mysteries. The experience my brother and I had with the rosary beads had proven that to me.

We were approaching the city. As I navigated the truck off the interstate I was surprised by flashing lights in my rearview mirror. As soon as I could, I pulled to the side of the road.

Don woke up to the sirens and flashing lights.

After checking our IDs and registration, the state trooper handed back my paperwork and gave me a warning to slow down.

I was grateful for not receiving a ticket and for the distraction from my thoughts.

Arriving in the city, we popped into Mom's house long enough for hugs before heading to Northwestern Westchester Hospital to pray for my grandmother.

"I hate hospitals," I confessed as we drove.

"Me too," Don agreed, "but thank God for all the staff, nurses, and doctors dedicating their lives to helping people."

"I know. But hospitals always seem so dark, and the patients seem so hopeless, except, of course, for the babies being born." I added, "And I hate the smell. I hate even the colors of the hallway, which are always some version of a terribly faded putrid sea-green color."

"Maybe it's because the angel of death is never far away in those places."

I had done much soul searching and praying just to get the courage to go to the hospital to visit my grandma. As we got closer to the hospital, I was having second thoughts about praying over my grandma and so was Don.

"There it is," I pointed as we approached the campus. "I'd forgotten how dreary and confusing this hospital parking lot was."

"Look," Don said with a laugh as he pointed at a sign:

LEFT, DOCTORS & STAFF ONLY.
LEFT FOR VISITORS PARKING.

I LAUGHED. "Hmm that is clear as a smoggy day in Los Angeles."

So, we turned—yep, you guessed it—LEFT.

We found the visitors' parking lot. I turned off the engine.

Turning to Don I said, "Let's pray."

He nodded.

"Thank you, Lord, for directing us to do what You would want us to do. In Jesus' name amen."

We signed in at the front desk of the hospital where the staff tried their best to make this lousy depressing place seem less dreary. We pinned our visitor's badges to our shirts, and the nice person working the front desk directed us to the area of the hospital where my grandma was staying. We walked the dingy halls trying to follow directions. Of course, we got lost.

"Another reason why I hate hospitals!" I exclaimed. "The layout is so confusing. Even the lines and arrows on the floor and walls make zero sense to me."

"I think we may be on the right floor," Don encouraged. "Let's check with the floor nurse."

"Oh yes," the nurse responded when we asked. "She's in room 30-404."

"Thank you," I said. "I am her grandson."

"I am sorry to say that she is in a non-responsive state," the nurse said. "Will you be, ok?" she asked.

I nodded.

I went in the room first and just held Grandma's hand for a few minutes. My heart was exploding. Anyone who knows me knows that I cry at a drop of a hat. Seeing Grandma hooked up to all kinds of machines and tubes, I was a heartbeat away from dissolving into tears.

"Dear God," I began to pray under my breath, "thank you for comforting Grandma and please don't let her have any pain."

I couldn't stand to think of her in any kind of pain. I told her that I loved her and wanted her to get better. Then I looked up and waved Don into the room to pray with me.

As Don walked into the room, he teared up. He did not know my grandma but has a grandma of his own—in fact, we had visited her in Chicago on our way to New York. Both of our grandmas were about the same age, and I'm sure seeing mine in this condition hit close to home for him.

I felt an urge to put my hands on my grandma's head and pray for her, but, oddly, I couldn't move my hands.

Don whispered, "Can we lay hands on your grandma and pray for healing?"

Something in me broke free. That's exactly what I had needed! I nodded and put my hands on her forehead. Don put his hands on her stomach.

"Dear God," I prayed, feeling a newfound boldness,

"thank you for comforting my grandma and, if it is your will, please heal her!"

"Thank you, God," Don said with authority, "for healing Rob's grandmother in Jesus' name."

Feeling faith well up inside me, I started praying the same thing: "Thank you, God, for healing my grandmother, in Jesus' name!"

Confidence pushed out my doubt and depression. I could tell that Don felt the same confidence as we continued praying.

"Praise you Lord for healing her, in Jesus' name!" we prayed in unison.

Suddenly, the monitoring machines went crazy, beeping and buzzing. My grandma's heart rate and oxygen levels were jumping. The monitors beeped and dinged. It sounded like an arcade filled with pinball machines.

Nurses rushed in.

"Leave the room now!" they demanded.

I squeezed my grandma's hand and told her that I loved her.

As Don and I left the room we claimed in unison: "We rebuke any evil or forces of darkness that are around my/Rob's grandmother, and we asked you, God, to put a protective hedge around her."

A few days later, my aunt answered the phone.

"Hello, is this Mary?"

"It is! Do you have news about my mother?"

"This is the patient coordinator from Northern Westchester Hospital. I am calling to inform you that your mother has awakened, and she is actually doing well."

"Thank God!"

"We see these things happen occasionally but not usually to a woman in her eighties. The doctor is recommending physical therapy for some weakness in her legs, but other than that she seems to be doing great. He's going to run a few more tests, but you can probably expect for her to be discharged in a few days."

"That's wonderful!"

My aunt hung up the phone in shock. She immediately called my mother a few blocks away. "Nina, how can Mom be unresponsive one moment and awake and coming home the next?" she asked.

Don and I walked in the front door as my mom was hanging up the phone after talking with my aunt.

She turned to us and said, "Your grandmother is coming home is a few days."

I was beside myself with joy. I could not stop giving thanks to God.

Don and I told her what had happened at the hospital with the monitors while we were praying for Grandma. As the word spread to other family members, everyone was amazed.

Grandma did come home. My uncle built her an exercise apparatus that she used diligently every day to build back the strength in her legs and arms. Within six months she was back to normal. She never even used a walker. She was an amazing woman!

She continued to exercise each day, and she

continued to pray every day, which I believe was the source of her strength. I loved her so!

She passed away a few years later when her heart gave out. No pain, no suffering.

I miss you, grandma!

I'll never forget how that summer started with a miracle.

And good thing, because I was about to walk into the most intense spiritual battles I had ever experienced.

4

A DAY IN HELL'S KITCHEN

THE NEXT MORNING, Don and I met up with our team at the Teen Challenge Center. Although I have never been to a battlefield, the neighborhood surrounding the center made me think of a war zone. There was smoke from burning cars and buildings. Graffiti was everywhere. There was a smell of human waste and urine and diesel fumes from buses.

The center was in the middle of a rough part of New York known as Hell's Kitchen. This was before it became the hip foodie destination it is today. Back then Hell's Kitchen was a dangerous place consisting of rows of blown out buildings, which some people suggested were damaged by landlords for the insurance. Other buildings were "shooting galleries," burned-out buildings where drug addicts and prostitutes congregated for their fixes and God knows what else.

This was where James had signed us up to work with street kids.

"What have we gotten ourselves into?" I mumbled to Don.

As we mingled with the other volunteers, I noticed that most of them looked like they were in shock, probably asking themselves the same question I had asked Don.

The team tasked with training us consisted of four local church pastors and two radio evangelists. The lead trainer Martin stood and got our attention. "Listen up, everyone," he said. "As you go into your assigned territories, there are strict rules you must follow."

Another leader, Orlando, chimed in. "I want to emphasize what Martin is saying about the seriousness of following all the rules. If anyone has a problem with that, they should leave the group now."

Martin spoke again. "Because we are going into dangerous places, please take this training very seriously. First, each assigned group will consist of three members who must stay together at all times."

"It's important to constantly keep an eye on each other," Orlando added.

"Also, each group will be assigned a partner group, also consisting of three people. In other words, two groups of three will be assigned to the same area, such as a block, a church, or a park."

"Each group must stay in sight of each other at all times," Orlando interjected.

"And most importantly," Martin said, wrapping up the rules, "all groups must return to the center two hours before dark." In an ominous voice he added, "Trust me, none of you want to be stranded in or around Hell's Kitchen after dark."

We nodded as terror welled up inside us.

Max, the group coordinator, pointed to me. "I am putting you and Don with Becki," he said.

Becki, it turns out, was an eighteen-year-old coed from Iowa. "I am so excited!" Becki squealed, "I've never worked with poor kids before. And this is my first visit to a big city."

"They don't get any bigger than the Big Apple," Don mumbled,

As Don and I reviewed the rules with her, Beckie twirled a lock of her hair. "Oh, I'm really not very good at following rules."

"Well," I said, "this is different because we can really get hurt here if we don't."

"Oh, I know," Becki sighed. "But it doesn't matter too much because God will take care of me."

The next few days Don and I were constantly reining Becki in from potentially dangerous situations.

"Becki, get back here," I screamed over the sounds of traffic.

"I'm telling the people in the cars about Jesus," Becki screamed back, waving me off.

She would run into stopped traffic at the red-light crossings and stick her head into the open windows of the idling cars.

"Really? Get back here," I screamed again.

"Let's go get her," Don commanded.

"What are you doing? Are you crazy?" Micah from

our partner group yelled as Don and I braved the traffic and escorted Becki back to the sidewalk.

"It's a miracle you didn't get run over," Jay, also from our partner group, yelled as he ran with Micah towards us.

"Are you nuts?" Micah turned to Becki. "You could have been pulled into a car or something worse."

"Becki, please do not run into traffic again," I pleaded, trying to stay calm.

"Okay, but God takes care of me," she smiled.

"Please, Becki, what you are doing is very dangerous, and you are putting all of us at risk. Try to be more careful."

"I'll try. But I know I am doing what I think God wants me to do. I'm sure He will keep me and all of us safe."

Don, Micah, and Jay were disheartened by her response and started down the sidewalk.

Becki followed, still defending herself. "Anyway, I've had some great responses from people. And I've never felt I was in any danger."

The next day we met at the center to get our assignments.

"Listen up," Max said to get our attention. "The kids you will be ministering to today have been recruited as mules for the local drug dealers."

"At least until the laws change," Martin added. "The local drug dealers use kids as young as nine years old to do their drug deliveries."

"How can they get away with that?" Becki asked almost in tears.

"They are taking advantage of the law," Martin explained, "because if these kids are caught, nothing much can be done to them legally because of their age."

"Of course," Orlando spoke up, "the drug dealers get these kids hooked on drugs to better control them."

"These kids are so impressionable," Becki said exasperatedly.

"They have no hope in their lives," Orlando said tenderly.

"And," Martin added, "that makes it easy for the drug dealers to recruit them with the lure of money, safety, and a feeling of belonging."

"What a tough situation," I thought out loud.

Orlando said, "Teen Challenge in NYC is working hard to get these young kids help and to try to get them on a better path."

Later that morning Don, Becki and I spotted a jittery group of young kids standing on the sidewalk. They each carried a black messenger bag and looked nervous.

Don pointed. "Let's go talk to them," he said.

We walked across the street.

"Hi guys, my name is Rob and—"

"Put your hands up!" A loud voice boomed.

Suddenly we were surrounded by a half dozen men wearing street clothes and brandishing badges.

"It's a drug sting!" Don exclaimed.

"You are interfering with the police," an officer boomed again, this time to Don, Becki, and me.

Another officer pushed us back. "Get out of here. This is police business."

"Because of you, we had to swoop in to get these kids earlier than planned," a third officer said to us.

"Leave the area NOW!" the first officer demanded.

We apologized sheepishly and left.

We'd just crossed the street when Don looked frantically from side to side.

"We lost Becki!" he yelled.

Panic set in.

"Who knows where she's wandered off to," Don grimaced.

"And what trouble she's gotten herself into," I added nervously.

We began frantically searching for her.

Seeing our partner group a few blocks away, I waved and caught Micah's attention. "Hey Micah!" I yelled. "Did you see which direction Becki went?"

"I'm not sure," he hollered back, heading in our direction. Then he pointed. "I saw someone heading toward the stack of blown out cars north of us."

As he drew near, Micah added, "Let me grab Jay and Ellen, and we'll help you search for her." He looked worried. "In the meantime, you and Don should stay put."

As Micah turned and ran back to his group, Don looked at me.

"Rob, I have a feeling—"

"—me, too. We can't wait 'til they get back," I said.

Without another word we raced in the direction in which Micah had pointed.

"Rob! I think that's her!" Don called out.

We had both caught a glimpse of someone turning a corner far ahead.

Without thinking we turned down the same alley.

We ran past twisted metal, burned out doorways, and busted furniture. Tall brick walls on either side of the alley blocked the sunlight.

"Watch out for all the needles and garbage piled everywhere," Don warned.

Like I hadn't noticed. And the place smelled like a sewer. "Any guardian angels we brought in with us just left us," Don said in an ill-attempt at humor.

"Yeah, I heard their wings flapping as they flew away," I laughed nervously. We now found ourselves in a very dark place. It was dark not only in a visual sense but in a spiritual sense. "Nothing good has happened in this ally in a really long time," I exhaled. "We didn't know Becki all *that* well," I mused. "Remind me again why we're doing this?"

"Shh. Listen." Don cocked his head.

We heard voices and laughter around the corner from where we were standing. Don and I look at each other before racing toward the voices. We turn a corner partially obstructed with stacked crates and garbage. Becki stood in the middle of the alley. Five men with chains around their waists and dew rags on their heads surrounded her. She was telling them about Jesus.

Each one looked like they just stepped out of prison. They had muscles on muscles and scars everywhere their skin was exposed. A strong scent of pot smoke hung in the air as well as the stench of stale beer and urine. A boom box blared deep base rap music. The kind of music that makes your entire body shake. Fear welled up in my heart.

Suddenly the guys started to close the circle tighter around Becki, bumping her body with theirs. They started to grab at her. Panic flashed in her eyes.

I lurched forward. Don was at my side. Everything seemed to move in slow motion as we busted into the group's circle. I'm not sure how we did it exactly but those hardened, muscle bond criminals seemed genuinely surprised when we broke through the circle.

We were surprised they didn't hear us coming. Thank God for the boom box.

"Let's go!" I screamed and grabbed Becki's wrist. But the men regrouping around us in an ever-tightening circle had a different idea.

"I rebuke this darkness in Jesus' name!" Don and I declared together at the exact same moment in the loudest voices we could muster. We felt the dark atmosphere parting like when Moses parted the Red Sea.

"Feel that?" I shouted.

"Our guardian angles flying back to our rescue!" Don laughed.

In an instant, every muscle-bound tough guy in the circle hunched over like someone had punched him in the stomach.

I still had Becki by the wrist. She, Don, and I walked right through the circle.

Who am I kidding? We ran for our lives through the circle away from those guys.

As I glanced back, I saw three of the guys struggling to stand with shocked expressions on their faces.

"What just happened?" one man yelled after us. "We don't even believe in Jesus!"

I'm not sure how we navigated all the twists and turns back out of the alleyway, but it seemed that in a heartbeat we were back on the main street with the sun shining down on us.

"Hallelujah!" Don cried out.

"Becki, we are too overwhelmed with joy to be angry with you," I said in a near chuckle.

"But we beg you to never again go down any of these alleys," Don insisted.

"Don't worry. I won't," she said without any hesitation.

5

THE HARLEM VOODOO BUILDING

THE NEXT DAY was another beautiful, hot summer day in New York. Don and I arrived at the meeting center still euphoric but shaken from yesterday's battle.

"Today your team will meet up with a local pastor of a small church in central Harlem," Orlando said to us.

As we headed out to minister, Becki decided to stay at the center.

"Hey, Rob and Don, help yourself to some donuts and coffee before you leave." Max said.

A moment later, Don and I were studying the map on the wall above the donut table. "It looks like we'll have to take the subway, then walk several blocks to get to the church," Don said.

It was still early morning when we got off the subway and began our walk. On the way, we noticed some local shop owners getting ready for the day, hosing down sidewalks in front of their shops and sweeping out their store fronts.

New York City shop owners take great pride in keeping their shops looking nice.

We found the people in Harlem to be very friendly. People passing by greeted us with smiles or a hello. In fact, among the neighborhoods in New York we visited on that trip, we found Harlem to be the friendliest.

"Wow, is this it?" I asked Don as we approached a small, dilapidated building. We walked in the front door and stood in the foyer. A decrepit bulletin board partially covered a humongous crack spreading in the plaster wall. Outdated choir practice notices and announcements of long-past church activities still hung on the board. A sign featuring big, red words caught our attention:

> Welcom Teen chalenge.!!!

Below the sign was pinned a crayon drawing of the congregation welcoming us to their church. I was overwhelmed with emotion. We later found out the kids of the congregation had made the signs. The amount of love poured into these drawings was evident.

We heard voices and looked up. The pastor and some members of the church approached us with big smiles on their faces. Don and I felt an instant connection as we were introduced. Then we were greeted with hugs and handshakes. These people were so warm and friendly, filled with hope, love, and Jesus that I seriously thought about applying for the children's ministry position posted on their activities board. Of course, reality had the upper hand and slapped me in the face—actually, Don slapped me—but I seriously considered it for a moment.

As we were getting to know some of the members over coffee and cookies, the pastor stood. "Don, Rob are you ready to head out?" he asked. "I pray we can help the kids in the neighborhood who have fallen into a life of drugs and crime."

"A *life* of? I whispered to Don. "Some of these kids are only nine years old."

"It's heart breaking," Don agreed.

We spent the morning in Harlem speaking with local teens and pre-teens about the dangers of dealing and using drugs.

"But what else can we do?" these kids asked in defeated voices.

We assured them that Teen Challenge could help them. They seemed interested.

For several hours, we stayed and explained how they could get help with schoolwork, clothing, and food. We emphasized that it *is* possible to get off drugs and the Teen Challenge was there to help. As the morning progressed, we made friends with these kids and began to see a glimmer of hope in their eyes. We prayed they would accept the help they so desperately needed.

"It's time for us to leave," Don reminded me.

"We have to get back," I told the pastor. "We volunteered to help with the setup of an outdoor concert."

"In Times Square?"

"Yes, how did you know?"

"Teen Challenge does a monthly Christian music concert in Times Square every summer," the pastor answered. "Who is performing tonight?"

"The Brooklyn Tabernacle Choir," I answered, "I'm really looking forward to it."

Some of the kids decided to walk Don and me to the subway station. On the way, as we approached a nondescript building, our escorts started to get jumpy and wanted to cross to the other side of the street.

"Hey guys what's wrong?" I asked.

"We don't want to walk past that building," one of the older teens answered.

"Why not?" Don asked.

"This building is a voodoo chapel, and a voodoo priestess lives there."

Don and I looked at each other with astonishment, and skepticism.

"Why do you think someone like that lives there?" Don asked.

"Look at the markings at the top of the windows and at the top of the building," another kid said.

"And look at all the writings on the brick walls," the first teenager added.

The two-story brownstone building was in horrid condition. I know nothing about voodoo, but the building felt evil.

"It sounds crazy, but it feels like this building is alive," Don whispered to me.

"I know," I agreed. "I am starting to feel like it's spewing out waves of fear."

"Maybe this is part of what's holding the local people down," Don suggested.

"Maybe these kids are messing with us," I said hopefully, trying to convince myself as well as Don. "And it's sparking our imaginations."

"I think we need to pray over the building," Don whispered.

"Yeah, I think you are right," I relented.

Approaching the building, we put our hands on the brick exterior, and I started to pray. "God, we ask that you remove the evil from this building and leave this neighborhood. We ask that goodness and godliness take its rightful place in the neighborhood and that the people of this area would be filled with hope."

It was a short simple prayer.

Don agreed with the prayer, and we finished together with the words, "in Jesus' name."

"Hey guys," Don addressed the teens who had come this far, "thanks for walking us to the station."

We ran the rest of the way to catch the next subway back to the center.

The next morning, Martin stood up to give out the assignments.

"Rob, Don, you guys head back to the Harlem area where you were yesterday. You will work with another small church there." He continued, "Rob, I would like you to help with their music worship program."

We arrived at the same subway station as the day before. As we ascended the stairs, we saw a few of the kids who had walked us to the subway the previous evening. As soon as they saw us, they came running up to us yelling. In their excitement, their words came out jumbled. Don and I just looked at each other. We had no idea what they were saying. They tugged on our shirts to follow them.

They pulled us with such emotion we couldn't help but go along with them. We realized they were taking us toward the church we visited the day before.

Then I saw it.

"Rob!" Don exclaimed. "Isn't that pile of rubble the same building we prayed over yesterday?" We now understood what the kids were saying.

"Yeah." A kid wearing a baseball cap flashed a big grin. "It's the voodoo building you both prayed over. It collapsed overnight."

"Hello boys," the church pastor said, surprising us as he approached from behind.

"The city has been trying to condemn that building for years."

"Well, we prayed over it yesterday that the evil would leave this area!" I said, glad to see our pastor friend.

"Praise Jesus!" the pastor exclaimed. "Well, your prayers worked because the priestess and her group are moving their activities to another part of the city. They are looking for another abandoned building to squat in."

Don and I looked at each other in amazement and wonder.

Today, the area of Harlem where the voodoo building collapsed, the little churches we visited are now a real estate hot spots where people are enjoying prosperity, peace, and joy.

Hmm, maybe I should have applied for the children's music ministry position after all!

I'll never forget that summer when we saw with our own eyes the power of God prevailing over evil.

A few weeks later, we made it back to Colorado.

And that's when things got *really* strange.

6

TAROT READERS AND SUPERNATURAL BATS

I LANDED a job at a local publishing company in Boulder. After work, I often headed to Boulder's Pearl Street mall with my guitar in tow.

Pearl Street, one of the first pedestrian malls in the country, consists of five blocks of shops, boutiques, eateries, and pubs. Most summer weekends, the mall turns into a circus of performing buskers showcasing their various talents and arts. On any given night, a performer can earn hundreds of dollars for a couple of hours of effort. Sword swallowers, jugglers, singers, and magicians cover the streets, creating a fun carnival atmosphere for tourists and locals alike.

I would arrive around six in the evening and start jockeying for a spot by the brick bank building or shoe store. Both buildings are perfect for singers because the architecture makes for great acoustics. I sounded like I was singing in a mini amphitheater.

As soon as I found a good spot, I would set out my

guitar case—not to collect money but to offer free literature about my Christian faith. I would serenade the summer crowds, playing and singing Christian worship and praise songs. In between songs, I often found myself in interesting conversations with people of all faiths and religions. Sometimes these conversations become quite invigorating.

Each evening, as the late-night hours approached, the entire mood of the mall would change. The exciting carnival feel would become eerie and dark.

A group of conga players often set up their drums near me. Their rhythms chased away the few families remaining in the area and invited in a more sexually driven atmosphere. As soon as they began to play, groups of bystanders would begin dancing and spinning in a frenzy.

Observing how this power of music moves people is extraordinary.

After the conga players, the tarot card readers would set up their stations and offer their services for a fee.

Most nights, as midnight approached, a group of young, self-described devil worshipers would seek me out with mocking, curses, and threats. For weeks, I tried responding to these kids with kindness but that only seemed to provoke them.

One day, I asked friends, church members, and family to pray for me during my weekend outings.

"Sure Rob," my pastor assured me. "I will get the prayer group to pray for the forces of light to overcome darkness, especially during the late evening hours."

The intensity of my own prayer life increased as well.

"Dear God," I prayed as the next weekend approached. "Allow goodness to overcome evil. Let Your light expel the darkness from the mall, my life, and the entire world."

I repeated this prayer all day long for several weeks, motivated by faith but also by fear.

In just a few weeks things on the mall seemed slightly better. The place started to feel a little less dark and a little less evil.

Was it just my hopeful imagination?

"WHAT ARE YOU DOING?" a group of tarot readers asked me one night around ten.

"I am singing praise and worship songs to the King of kings and Lord of lords," I explained. (I was young and zealous so I couldn't just tell them I was singing, could I?)

"No not that," one of them answered. "We are not talking about your singing, which we've been suffering through all summer. We want to know what you are doing to block our gifts of reading the cards," another said.

"What am I doing to make you so angry?" I snapped. "All I'm doing is singing songs. I'm singing about my Christian faith."

"No, we said it's not your singing," the group leader snapped back. "What is preventing us from doing any readings? You are blocking our spiritual connections."

"We all get the premonition that you are the cause," a woman in the group pointed her finger in my face. "*You* are the blockage."

"Well," I responded, "a group of my friends and I have been praying for light to chase the darkness away from the mall. Are your gifts from the light or from the darkness?"

Many in the group fell all over themselves trying to answer me at the same time.

"We get our gifts from the powerful place of the underworld," one woman said defensively.

"Our readings are not from darkness, so you are mistaken," someone else barked.

"We demand that you stop whatever you are doing to block our gifts," the leader said forcefully.

"I am no expert," I said, "but the Old Testament talks about the evils of soothsaying."

Several members of the group murmured.

"Do you classify yourselves as soothsayers?" I asked mockingly. I was young and zealous and not very tactful. "You just told me your readings are not from the powers of darkness. If that is true, you should have nothing to worry about."

As I taunted them, my conscience started to bother me because of the way I was treating these people.

"I don't mean to make light of your gifts," I said, weakly apologizing. "My prayers to God are only to have the powers of darkness be expelled by the true light."

They responded by giving me hand gestures and spewing hexes and curses. One by one they all turned and left. I continued to endure harassment from this group each time I sang on the mall. But something interesting started to materialize. Their presence started to dwindle. Then the group moved their readings toward the opposite end of the mall. But even at that distance, they seemed aware of me, and about an hour into my singing they would pack up and leave the mall altogether. In an angry huff, they would walk past me giving me finger gestures and yelling, "Stop blocking us."

This happened night after night.

Wow! Increasingly, I was learning that this prayer stuff wasn't just for Sunday school.

I BEGAN to share with friends who had been praying for me that God was answering their prayers.

"I'm seeing God really take hold of people at the mall," I frequently told them. "You can feel the difference in the air—especially during the late-night hours!"

"Rob, could I join you some weekend?" one friend asked. He wasn't the only one. Soon people from my church were asking to participate too, either by singing or by talking with bystanders while others sang.

"Yes. yes. yes, I would love the company," I always responded.

I was especially excited when my friend Angie asked to join me. Angie had a beautifully trained voice, and she and I had performed together a few times mainly in churches. One of my favorite experiences had been performing with her as an opening act for a contemporary Christian rock band on the CU Boulder campus. It had been an exciting opportunity for both of us!

When we started performing together on the mall, it was no surprise that we had lots of fun—and people visiting Pearl Street Mall loved it as well.

Angie truly has a great voice, and before long large crowds formed each night she was there. People clapped and cheered after each song and commented how they loved the words of our songs. We had positive and interesting conversations with people in the crowds about everything from music to religion. It was a fabulous time. Until one evening when the darkness returned.

The families and tourists had left the area, and a new crowd populated the mall. I noticed the conga players, who I hadn't see in a while, setting up their little stage to do whatever they would do. I felt something different spiritually that night.

As midnight approached, a group of bikers roamed the mall looking for trouble. It was very unusual.

One of the fortune tellers I hadn't seen recently was setting up her station. As the bikers passed her, she waved them over and began speaking with them. Two of the guys looked over at Angie and me. These guys were big and looked mean. They started walking towards us. Angie was still singing and directing her attention to a group of people on our right. She had yet to see the men approaching.

"Lord," I prayed quickly. "It has been some time since I practiced my karate. Please help my skills and protect us." A strange prayer, but that's what I prayed.

I looked up and these two guys were about five feet away from Angie with smirks on their faces. When they reached for Angie's arms, I dropped my guitar to jump in front of her. Suddenly, I saw their arms being pulled behind their backs. Even though no one was anywhere near them, both these guys were spun around right in front of my eyes.

Then, to my amazement, they appeared to be escorted—by no one!—away from us towards the opposite end of the mall. Just like that, they were gone. The remaining bikers said something to the tarot card reader, then turned on their heels and left the mall.

"Wow!" I turned to Angie. "What just happened? Did you see that?"

"See what?"

"Something—our angels—protected us from two tough guys and forced them out of the mall!" I said, almost hyperventilating. "And they just left us alone! Without anyone even touching them!"

"Well, I didn't see anything, but our angels are mighty, glorious creatures," Angie assured me as she grabbed more sheet music.

That was just the beginning. The night got even more bizarre. About an hour after the miracle with the two bikers, I noticed a group of teenagers I knew were self-proclaimed satanists. They were huddling in a circle with their leader, Sage, a drug dealer in his early thirties.

I hadn't seen these kids for weeks.

I glanced at them as they pointed and laughed at Angie and me. Sage yelled something, and they stopped pointing. Holding hands, they began making ominous chanting sounds. As their chants became louder and louder, a buzzing sound arose.

In an instant they stopped. Devoid of emotion and movement, they stared at Angie and me. They looked like zombies with blank, empty eyes.

My spirit churned in the pit of my stomach. I said a quick prayer and then told Angie I felt something weird was going on and asked if she would pray also. I looked up. Out of nowhere, two huge bats with enormous wingspans appeared and flew down the Pearl Street Mall right toward us.

I looked around frantically. People were paying no attention, as if giant bats were a nightly occurrence, which they were not.

At that moment, both conga drum players stopped drumming and stared at the bats. They began chanting too.

I focused my attention back on the bats. By now they were circling in front of us. Visitors and performers continued milling around enjoying the Colorado summer evening as if nothing were happening.

It was a surreal moment to say the least.

Suddenly, the two bats stopped circling and hovered about ten feet away, facing Angie and me. They reminded me of how hawks hover in the wind of an approaching storm.

Suddenly one of them made a beeline straight for my face. I froze with fear.

"Jesus is Lord and I rebuke this in Jesus' name!" I somehow yelled at the top of my voice.

The bat kept coming.

Pow!

He slammed into an invisible wall like a bird against a clean window. Retreating several feet, he shook himself, then came at us again at full speed.

"Jesus is Lord, and I rebuke this in Jesus' name!" I shouted again at the top of my voice.

Bam!

He bounced off the invisible barrier again.

The second bat joined the first. They both flew full force straight at us.

Slam!

To the naked eye there was nothing in front of us but open air. And yet apparently a spiritual force field had been placed in front of us to protect us from these creatures.

Something—or Someone—was not letting these two bats get close to us.

Wow! Angie and I started laughing hysterically. Praise melodies we had never sang before began flowing from our lips.

The bats tried a few more times before giving up. In an instant, they were gone.

"Did you see that?" we both asked each other. "Incredible!"

Once again, a spiritual power had been given to us to shield us from dark forces that did not like what we were doing on the Pearl Street Mall—forces that had been trying to intimidate us into running away.

It hadn't worked.

Sage and his crew had dumbfounded looks on their faces. They were shaking their heads and spewing obscenities. In disgust they all headed toward Sage's van and left the mall not to return for the rest of the evening.

I thought about chasing them down to see if I could get more details about the bats, but Angie did not think it was such a good idea. Besides, we both suddenly felt exhausted.

We decided to pack up and call it a night. We laughed and sang praises to our Lord until we both arrived at each of our homes safely.

Several weeks later, I saw Sage and his group back on the mall. I noticed that the number of kids in his gang was much smaller.

7

THE HOUSE GUEST FROM HELL

LATER THAT SUMMER OF 1985, my housemate, Roger, joined me to sing on the mall.

We sang for many hours, but not successfully. We sang out of tune, made musical mistakes, and didn't really connect with anyone.

Toward the end of the night, a guy named JD came over to where we were singing. He stopped just to hang out and listen, which he did on and off most of the night. This guy seemed like a young homeless person. He was in his late twenties or early thirties and had long straggly blond hair, wore torn blue jeans, and carried a ratty old green backpack.

He listened as hecklers interrupted our singing, trying to start a debate. Each time, we responded by explaining our beliefs, but anything we said just pushed people's buttons, making them agitated.

Sometimes they screamed and yelled at us:

"Why do you believe the fairy tales of Christianity?"

"You all are idiots to believe this stuff."

"Look at all the wars your precious religion started."

"F*** you and your religion."

They got in our faces and mocked us.

Usually, I get energized when confronted and challenged, but for some reason on that strange night, the attacks exhausted and depressed Roger and me. Because we felt so wiped out, I decided it would be best to pack up a little early and call it a night.

JD noticed we were getting ready to leave.

"Hey guys," he spoke up. "I really enjoyed listening to your debates tonight and was wondering if I could ask a few questions. I just got out of prison for buying pot, and I'm curious about a few things."

"Wow! I hope you're doing, okay?" I responded.

"Well, actually, I have no place to stay and was wondering if you knew of a place I could crash for the night."

"You can stay with us tonight," Roger offered.

"Wait a minute," I protested, upset Roger had offered our place without asking me.

I am all about helping people, but I've worked with the homeless enough to know you must be smart about each situation. There are extremely dangerous people living on the streets. Some are mentally ill. And every one of them has a heartbreaking story, whether it's true or not. Having a tender heart and wanting to help—but without having the proper training—can be a dangerous combination. Shelters, on the other hand, have the expertise, facilities, and resources for properly and safely helping those in need.

I suggested a nearby shelter instead.

"The Boulder shelter is full, and I really want to talk about my beliefs with you," JD pleaded.

Ignoring my inner warning of danger, I begrudgingly agreed. We packed everything up and headed to our apartment, which was a fifteen-minute walk from the mall. On the way, JD asked all sorts of questions about sorcery and demon worship. We explained our understanding of the origins of demons and how fallen angels try to imprison human souls.

JD seemed very receptive of the descriptions of good and evil and how Jesus came to destroy evil and death. He asked why we call Jesus the Savior and the Son of God. Both Roger and I love talking about the Bible, and excitedly explained that God sent Himself in human form to the earth to destroy evil by taking on humankind's punishment for our sins. One day, we added, He will restore the human condition back to our glorified state where there is no suffering or evil of any kind. We explained when God does come back to right all the wrongs done on Earth, evil and darkness will be banished forever.

JD seemed like a sponge, and we couldn't wait to get home to crack open the Bible and get deeper into the theology of Christianity.

I started to relax. Obviously, I'd been paranoid about helping this guy out.

The three of us talked for an hour or so after arriving home. JD asked very insightful questions and together the three of us would try to find what the Bible had to say about the issues. Throughout the discussion, JD seemed very concerned about what was going to happen to the demons.

We made some coffee, frozen pizzas, and popcorn and had a very stimulating conversation over dinner.

As the evening wore on, JD yawned every few minutes, and my eyes drooped with exhaustion.

"It looks like we are running out of steam," Roger said.

"Yep," I answered, "I think it's time for me to call it a night."

"Let me get you some blankets," Roger said to JD. "You can sleep on the couch down here in the living room. The bathroom is the second door from the right past the kitchen."

"Can you help me get established with the local shelter in the morning?" JD asked, now sounding half asleep.

"Sure," Roger assured. "The Boulder shelter has some great services, and people to help you with whatever you need."

I headed upstairs to call it a night. Exhausted, I fell asleep as soon as my head hit my pillow. About an hour later, I was awoken by the sound of Gregorian chanting.

Had I left my radio on?

Someone continued to whisper the chants softly. The voice sounded odd, like one voice layered over itself. The hair on the back of my neck stood up.

I'm probably hearing my neighbor's music coming through the air vents, I rationalized and managed to drift back asleep. Not long after that I was awakened again.

What is that light shining in my eyes? I wondered as a light seeped from under the bathroom door.

In the dark, any amount of light seems like a spotlight—and the small amount seeping under the door illuminated my entire room.

Agitated, I said under my breath, "Why don't they turn down their music! I can still hear it through the vent."

As the chanting grew louder and louder my adrenaline kicked in, and I became more alert. I realized it was no longer layers of the same voice. Many voices, all dark and guttural, had joined in chanting in a language I did not recognize.

What the heck is going on!

I tried to get out of bed to investigate, but I discovered I could not move. I couldn't lift my limbs. I felt as if I were buried in sand.

Stay calm... I ordered myself, but I was shaking, noticing a weird sense of evil filling my bedroom.

I opened my mouth to yell at whoever was in the bathroom, but no sound came out. Fear gripped my soul.

I must be dreaming. It's just a nightmare.

But it was no dream. JD's voice pierced the night air. "Don't fight him!" he yelled through the bathroom door.

I wanted to wretch.

"The forces of darkness will be here soon to set all of us free."

"What the heck are you talking about?" I tried to scream the words, but they came out in a whisper.

He didn't answer.

As an eerie silence enveloped the room like a wet

blanket, smoke began seeping out from under my bathroom door. *Is the house on fire?* Wide-eyed and shaking, I had no idea what to do next. The smoke seeping into my bedroom began to shape itself into a human form.

Fueled by fear, I struggled with all my might to get up, but I still couldn't move. Trapped in my bed, I lay there wide awake. I was acutely aware it was no nightmare but a full-fledged spiritual attack.

Focus away from the fear and toward faith in Jesus, I told myself.

Terrified, I try to pray, *Jesus, help me.*

I forced myself to think of Bible verses I had memorized over the years and recite them over and over in my head. I recited in my mind as 2 Timothy 1:7: *God has not given me a spirit of fear but of power, love and sound mind.*

I remained terrified and powerless. I struggled now with my hatred toward JD for bringing this evil into my house. My head was spinning, and I felt woozy; I wondered if I was crazy.

God has not given me a spirit of fear but of power, love and sound mind, popped into my thoughts again.

Put on the full armor of God, so that you can take your stand against the devil's schemes.... Stand firm then, with the belt of truth buckled around your waist, with the breastplate of righteousness in place, and with your feet fitted with the readiness that comes from the gospel of peace...take up the shield of faith, with which you can extinguish all the flaming arrows of the evil one (Eph 6:10, 14-16 NIV)

Scripture continued flowing effortlessly through my mind.

The smokey fog had completely filled my room. I felt like I was suffocating.

And to my intense horror, the human form emerged out of the fog only a few feet from the foot of my bed.

Concentrate, Rob. Push aside the fear and concentrate! Help me, Jesus! I mouthed to myself.

I continued reciting Bible verses in my mind:

> *God has not given me a spirit of fear but of power, love and sound mind.*

> *Put on the full armor of God, so that you can take your stand against the devil's schemes.... [My] feet [are] fitted with the readiness that comes from the gospel of peace, [and I] take up the shield of faith with which [I can] extinguish all the flaming arrows of the evil one."*

I alternated between the verses as I painstakingly forced myself to ignore the all-encompassing fear and hold to my faith.

Jesus, help me! I prayed while trembling. My mind was racing. *Doesn't God through Jesus Christ and the Holy Spirit live inside me?*

Then something deep inside me began to stir and bubble, like something percolating in the pit of my stomach. Stronger and stronger my spirit rose, until it felt like a rushing river was emerging from the center of my stomach.

I'd never felt Him as powerfully as I was feeling Him now.

Shaking, sweating and sick to my stomach, I silently said, *Thank You, Lord.*

It felt as if my head and body were being squeezed between two giant vise grips as warring forces battled over my flesh, soul, and spirit. It was as though one force was trying to crush and decimate me while the other force propped me up, giving me a supernatural strength.

A new verse exploded in my thoughts: *Say to the Lord, my refuge and fortress, my God in whom I trust."* (Psalms 91:2 NABRE). And then I thought of: *No evil shall befall you, no affliction come near your tent.* (Psalm 91:10 NABRE).

I try to say aloud, "For he will command his angels concerning you to guard you in all your ways." (Psalm 91:11 NIV).

Suddenly, an intense thought filled my head. Was it my voice? Was it something else? I do not know. But permeating my thoughts, filling my head and consciousness were these words: "Rob, say it! Say it out loud. Speak the name of the one who gives you strength." I couldn't believe what I was hearing. I was frozen, but then I heard it a second time like someone shouting with a bull horn in my ear: "Rob, say it! Say it out loud. Speak the name of the one who gives you strength."

I was paralyzed with horror as I looked up at the smoky figure hovering above me. *Rob, I command* myself, *you must concentrate all your strength on speaking out loud.*

"God has not given me a spirit of fear but of power, love and sound mind," I manage to say in a faint whisper.

"God has not given me a spirit of fear but of power, love and sound mind " I whispered a little more loudly. I was exhausted but encouraged.

Suddenly, I felt a force like stampeding bulls welling up inside of me. No, not bulls! It was as if I had the strength of a thousand angels! I sat up, and in the loudest commanding voice I could muster, shouted, "I rebuke this show of darkness in Jesus' name!"

I repeated this rebuke ten times or so, and each time I shouted in an unnaturally loud voice.

"Leave this place and my home in Jesus' name!" The words continued to flow out of me like a raging river running out of my mouth.

What happened next reminded me of the 1960s TV show *I Dream of Jeannie*. When the genie returns to her bottle, she turned into smoke that is then sucked quickly into the bottle. That's EXACTLY what happened to the smoke in my room. Immediately after I shouted, "Leave this place and my home in Jesus' name!" all the smoke and the smoky figure hovering above me was sucked back under the bathroom door and disappeared. In a flash, the bathroom light turned off, and I heard JD running down the stairs toward the living room.

By then it was six in the morning. My mishap with the smoke and the underworld had taken the entire night.

"What is going on? What just happened?" Roger

asked as he rushed out of his bedroom and into the hallway. He stood there with a dazed look on his face as JD ran down the stairs, grabbed his stuff, and stumbled out the front door.

Roger, almost hyperventilating, stuttered, "This… this entire night, something paralyzed me in my bed. No matter what I did, I could not move. I… I struggled all night to get out of bed but could not."

"I know. I know!"

"And there was dark singing like a chorus of demons, and all I could do was pray against this evil!"

"Believe me, Roger, I know!" I said.

"I kept quoting 'God has not given me a spirit of fear but of power, love and sound mind.' And then, after hearing you scream Jesus' name, I broke free and sat up and immediately jumped out of bed to see if you were alright. Instead, I saw JD with a twisted, horrified look on his face jumping down the stairs like he was being chased by a ferocious dog."

I wanted to tell Roger that I'd experience the same battles. I wanted to tell him God had given me exact same Bible verse to fight the enemy. But I was exhausted and could merely nod my head.

I was free but very shaken.

Relieved that JD was out of our house, we praised God for protecting us through the night.

I moved out as soon as the lease was up. That place was never really the same after the JD incident. I moved into my own space, a studio apartment in the Table Mesa neighborhood in South Boulder.

I remained rattled for a long time, having experienced

the realities of such darkness, but I'm forever grateful that God delivered me from that horrible experience and is always by my side. I never again invited any "street person" into my house and, sadly, lost much of my compassion for them as well.

After this incident I noticed I had more thoughts of fear: fear of letting God down, fear of not being good enough. I deflected these accusations by meditating on Scripture that reminded me to fear not.

But it remained a daily struggle for some time.

8

ROCK AND ROLL, THE OCCULT, AND JOSH'S STORY

EARLY AUTUMN, after my awful experience with JD, a man named Darron joined our church with his family. During this time, several preachers were developing interesting ideas to reach the youth. A few months later, Darron founded a Christian radio show discussing rock and roll music, and the influence of the occult on this genre. His show was designed as a call-in format where he often argued about how rock and roll can influence kids to experiment with occultism and satanism. He discussed lyrics of popular groups such as Black Sabbath, AC/DC, Blue Oyster Cult, and others to support his talking points. He concluded these bands were tools and spokesmen used by the forces of darkness to lure kids into the underworld of evil. Apparently, he touched a nerve with kids because his radio show was a hit.

Darron also traveled around to local churches and college campuses to speak, and his presentations always packed the venues whenever he spoke. Sometimes he attracted kids wanting to argue with him in support of their favorite bands. The kids argued that bands use occult imagery and lyrics as entertainment and nothing more.

At first, I was on the kids' side and skeptical of Darron's hypothesis. As a musician I think most of these bands use the imagery of evil as a form of entertainment and are not purposefully setting out to be recruiters for the evil one. These guys see what they do as a money-making business. But when I would sing on the streets, I continued to have brushes with darkness. I met many kids either living on the streets or hanging out with kids living on the streets who idolized these bands and proclaimed themselves as satanists.

It was my run-ins with Sage that finally pushed me over to Darron's point of view. Sage told me flat out that his goal was to have all these kids worshiping Satan, and there was nothing I nor anyone else could do to stop him. As I've mentioned before, Sage was a leader of most of the kids living or hanging out on the streets. He was also a self-proclaimed worshiper of Satan and used music to lure kids into his world. In fact, Sage and the teens who followed him had tattoos and wore clothing marked with symbols of evil and the names and logos of the bands Darron had mentioned.

Darron was getting the youth and singles groups in our church fired up to preach against these bands. One afternoon after church a group of young adults came up to me as I was leaving.

"Rob, would you like to join us Saturday?" the youth

leader asked. "A group of us are going to the Blue Oyster Cult and Black Sabbath concert."

"Why are you going to this concert?" I asked.

"We're curious why these bands are so appealing to concertgoers," he explained, adding, "We are not going to attend the concert. We're going to hang outside and ask teens if they have been influenced by these bands to explore the occult and darkness."

He beamed. This outing had been his idea.

"It does sound intriguing to me, but—"

"Great! We will meet at the church to pray before we go."

They all turned and left, high fiving each other before I could finish my sentence:

"—I don't think it's such a good idea."

Oh boy, what did I just agree to?

Little did I know that across town a story was unfolding. It was a story of a young man named Josh, and our paths were about to intersect, shaking heaven and hell in the process.

JOSH WAS A TYPICAL TWENTY-FIVE-YEAR-OLD GUY. He was stuck in a nowhere job pumping gas at the local gas station on Colfax. He lived to drink beer and play Nintendo, even though his lack of motivation really got on his girlfriend's nerves. His other passion in life was listening to hard rock and heavy metal music. These bands and their music were his identity.

After a night of heavy partying, Josh decided to make

his way home in his nineteen sixty-nine Firebird. Josh's goal was to someday restore his Firebird to showroom condition but had not gotten around to it. His Nintendo playing and beer drinking seemed to keep getting in the way of the restoration.

Driving home, he noticed he was just about out of gas. He had only five bucks on him, but it was enough to get him home and make it back and forth to work until payday.

He pulled his half gray, half red Firebird into the next gas station he saw. It was one of those off-brand gasoline stations with the cheap gas.

He pulled up to the first available gas pump with AC/DC blaring out his car speakers. He parked the car and got out to put his five dollars of gas into his car. Removing the gas cap, he noticed a bald tattooed guy walking towards him.

"Hi," the stranger spoke. "Allow me to introduce myself. They call me Sage," he said sticking out his hand. Josh shook his hand as Sarge continued, "I'm looking to upgrade my car speakers and yours sound phenomenal."

"Yeah, they sound pretty incredible, don't they?" Josh agreed. "I found them through a mail order business I saw listed in one of my car magazines."

"And I admire your choice of music," Sage added. "I love AC/DC. I'm a big heavy metal music buff."

"Really? Me too," Josh said.

"The energy that comes from heavy metal bands is intoxicating and so freeing," Sage said with a grin.

"I guess I never thought about it," Josh mused, "but you're right. That's exactly how they make me feel."

"Josh, don't you ever wonder why these bands affect you so deeply? These bands tap into the power of the underworld and *that* is why they are so successful. That is why they move people so deeply, especially people who are fed up with the illusion of being good and trying to live a good life."

Sage paused.

"That sounds like me," Josh admitted sheepishly. "All my life I've tried being a good guy and doing the right thing and where has it gotten me?"

"And the music makes you feel powerful, doesn't it? Powerful and primal?"

Josh nodded, surprised at what he was hearing.

"That is exactly what it does for me," Sage answered in a euphoric voice. "So, what are you doing Saturday night?"

"I don't know. Why?"

"I have an extra ticket to the Blue Oyster Cult and Black Sabbath concert. I don't want the ticket to go to waste, and I would love to have a major fan as yourself use it."

"Yes! I would love to go!" Josh yelled, feeling like he'd just won a million dollars.

Handing a card to Josh Sage said, "A bunch of kids are meeting up at my house and heading to the concert together. Why don't you join us? The address is on the card. It's the gray house off the Pearl Street Mall on Pine. Get there early so you have some time to meet the others."

"Totally!" Josh assured him. "Thanks again, man." Josh waved as Sage returned to his van and left.

On Saturday, Josh left straight from work wearing a heavy metal T-shirt to meet up at Sage's house. Josh had no trouble finding the house. It was an old Victorian that needed much repair, as did most of the houses on the street. The brown and gray paint on the house was weathered and peeling. The front porch groaned under dilapidated chairs and sofas that seemed to have been through heavy partying. The glow of candles in the window caught his attention as he approached the front door, which opened before he had a chance to knock.

"Welcome to the dark side. I'm Samantha."

Josh was greeted with a big hug by a woman wearing tight ripped jeans and a clingy white shirt. On the shirt was the graphic of a pentagram, a five-pointed star used in dark magic in some circles.

"Please join the rest of the group in the candlelit circle to give thanks to the forces of darkness," Samantha said, pointing to the living room.

The invitation to join the circle made Josh feel uneasy. He wasn't a religious guy, but he knew enough about good and evil to have an uncomfortable feeling about this entire, strange situation.

"Look what Darkness has brought you in just a few days," Samantha said seductively as she took him by the hand. "You are going to a great concert, all expenses paid, and you are holding hands with a beautiful girl who has a crush on you."

Samantha's intoxicating flirtation with Josh wiped out any hesitation he had about joining her.

Oh, the powers of a seduction!

Samantha brought him a beer and offered him

some food. Josh took both as he was both famished and very thirsty for a beer. No one mentioned to Josh that the food was laced with psychedelic mushrooms and weed. In fact, all the food and drink were laced with drugs.

"Josh, welcome, I'm glad you made it," Sage said approaching his guest. "Please join me and my friends in the family circle to thank the powerful dark forces for giving us such a great life."

Josh's skin crawled with all the talk of dark powers and the underworld. But Samantha's hand was warm in his. And the beer tasted so good. *What the heck, I can't turn down free beer, free food, free concert tickets, and of course lots of attention from Samantha,* he thought to himself. He walked into the living room. About twenty kids ranging from mid-teens to mid-twenties stood in a circle around a five-foot pentagram painted on the wooden floor.

Samantha caressed Josh and put her arm around his waist and guided him into the circle.

"We love darkness," the group chanted.

"Take us as gifts to the underworld."

"A life following evil has no rules, no laws, and we do what we want." Their voices grew louder. "We give our devotion to the lord of the darkness. And he will give us whatever we want in this world."

The wind began to blow against the windowpanes, the lights dimmed, and the candles went out.

"Choose now!" Sage commanded. "Choose evil."

Josh's head was spinning, he couldn't keep his balance. Overwhelmed, he passed out and hit his head hard on the floor. His mind was instantly engulfed in blackness.

And then silence.

"Josh! Wake up or you're going to miss the concert," Sage said, nudging him.

Josh, sprawled on a step of the arena, didn't stir. Not wanting to miss the concert, Sage left Josh to fend for himself and ran toward the arena.

Josh opened his eyes and rubbed his head. Lifting his head, he looked around. He had no idea how he'd gotten from the house to the arena. He felt woozy as foggy memories of the past few hours began coming back to him.

"God," he prayed out loud, still struggling to sit up, "show me if you care what happens to me! Just give me one sign that you are real, and I will turn my back on all this crazy darkness stuff!" As Josh pushed himself up from the steps and stood weakly, a homeless guy jumped him and tried to pull Josh's jacket away from him. Josh spun around and punched the guy square in the face. The man crumbled to the ground like a graham cracker.

"Great! Just *great!*" Josh exclaimed. Then he thought, *I had better get out of here before I get into a jam with the cops.*

He saw his hand had begun to swell and feared he must have broken it. Nausea hit as excruciating pain moved from his fist up his entire arm.

The pain, the night, his emptiness all seemed to converge. It broke him.

"THAT?" he yelled heavenward. "That was Your sign? Not even You care about me. I don't know why You or anyone else would pay attention to what happens to me."

He sank back onto the step and buried his face in his hands.

9

THE INTERVENTION

OUR GROUP ARRIVED at the arena parking lot about an hour before the concert started. We split up into small groups. My friend Don and two other guys, Ben and Jerome, were part of my group. We thought we were early, but crowds of people rushed past us to get inside the arena, anticipating a great concert.

"Most of these people do not want anything to do with us," Don said to me, stating the obvious.

"They didn't come here to discuss their religious beliefs or the threat of heavy metal music to their souls," I answered.

"And who can blame them? They paid big bucks to be here tonight."

"I feel like we're intruding, uninvited, on someone else's turf," I added, feeling nervous.

"Well, we're here now. I just pray some good will come from all this," Don answered.

I nodded.

Ben, who was wearing a Jesus Saves T-shirt, joined us. "Hey, let's go talk to those guys," he said. He pointed toward a few men huddled in the back corner of a nearby industrial building.

Jerome, who had also joined us, nodded in agreement.

"I don't think it's a good idea to leave the lighted parking area," I protested.

"Rob, we might as well give it a try because we are not doing any good here," Don said, siding with Ben and Jerome.

We walked across the parking lot toward the group of guys. Our surroundings were getting darker and darker as we left the well-lit arena parking area. As we approached the area, I felt something was wrong. The hair on the back of my neck started to stand up.

Angel of the Lord, surround us with Your protection, I prayed silently, feeling scared.

As we approached, we could see that one of the men sat on the top concrete step as if he were sitting on a throne. The other two men, who were lower than him, as though they were his subjects, were letting blood drip from their cut fingers into dixie cups.

I felt nauseated.

The leader was chanting gibberish over them and giving praise to the power of darkness. Suddenly he stopped and pointed a finger at us. "What is the meaning of this intrusion on unholy ground?" he growled.

"We are here to share the good news of the gospel of Jesus Christ," Ben said boldly.

"Is that so? Then please approach and tell me all about this so-called good news," the leader commanded.

"What a great opportunity!" Ben whispered to our group.

"How exciting!" Jerome said.

"I'm not so sure," I added, but too late.

My two friends ran ahead of Don and me and started chatting with the two guys holding dixie cups. These guys skillfully maneuvered my friends, so their backs were against the cold concrete wall. My friends, unaware, remained focused on telling these guys all about Jesus.

Jerome and Ben didn't notice they were trapped.

Don and I could see what was happening and started running faster toward our friends.

Just as we arrived, we heard the throne guy say, "Proceed" to his two cohorts.

"Here we go again," Don said to me.

"Stop!" I said in loud voice, being obedient to the Spirit welling up inside me. The throne guy looked at me as did his two chums. He waved at the two guys to stand down. I saw one of them put a knife into his hoodie pocket.

"Don! Rob! We're trapped!" Ben hollered, sounding terrified.

The leader kept looking at me. I stared directly into his eyes. His scarred face and black lifeless eyes were crusted over with hatred.

"In Jesus' name, let my friends go!" I said holding my stare.

He stood up from his throne and took two steps

toward me. This guy was over six feet tall and all muscle. He again stopped and stared at me.

"Would you like to hear the story of how Jesus conquered the power of darkness?" I asked, still holding my stare.

A few seconds passed without a word. It seemed like an eternity. He just stared at me in silence.

I feel like I am glowing, I thought. *It feels like an intense heat is engulfing me.* A soft amber glow lit up the area.

"Would you like to hear the story of how Jesus conquered the power of darkness?" I asked again.

Silence.

"Oh, I see you're a man of few words," I said, feeling cocky. "Maybe you didn't know Jesus conquered the power of darkness."

More silence.

"I rebuke the power of darkness!" I cried out, spinning around, and pointing to the two men blocking my friends. "Release my friends in Jesus' holy name!"

The Spirit exploded power out of me.

"Free them in Jesus' name!" Don said, power exploding from him as well.

Immediately the two guys backed away from Ben and Jerome, who ran over to where Don and I stood.

Ben and Jerome just stared at me like I had two heads. The throne guy, still glaring at me with empty eyes, took another step forward.

My friends moved closer, flanking me on each side. We stood shoulder to shoulder, terrified, shaking but emboldened by what had just taken place. Still, we were not a very menacing group.

The throne guy broke his stare to look at my arms, then back into my eyes. Don was also staring at my arms. So were Jerome, Ben, and the two bullies.

"I know the story of your God," the throne guy growled, "and the story of my god. I choose darkness. Now leave this place."

"It's never too late to change your decision," I said. "Jesus accepts anyone who believes in Him and asks Him for help and forgiveness. Here take this." I stretched out my hand, offering a pocket New Testament.

Without a word, he took it!

We turned, leaving the three men behind us as we quickly returned to the arena.

"Praise God! Did you see that?" Ben said to Don.

"Hey, did you feel anything?" Don asked me.

"I felt the presence of the Holy Spirit," I answered, "and a kind of heat all around me, like a weird adrenaline rush or something."

"You looked like a giant compared to that guy," Jerome said.

"What? But I'm not. I'm five six."

"No, man. Your arms were the size of tree trunks, and you looked like you were six feet tall," Don insisted.

"Wait. So, you're telling me while I was talking to throne guy, I had huge muscles?" I said in amazement.

"Yes!" Ben responded.

"Well, thank you Lord!" I responded, with a grateful heart.

Exhausted, we headed back to our cars to call it a

night. No one had any more strength to do anything else that evening.

But God had His own idea about how this night would end.

While walking through the parking lot in search of our cars, we stumbled upon a guy leaning up against a Jeep. He was clearly in a lot of pain. His eyes were wild, like those of a caged animal.

"Hey man, are you ok?" I asked.

"No, not really," he groaned. "I was just jumped by some guy, and I think I broke my hand."

"What's your name?" Jerome asked.

"My name is Josh. I am not doing so good. I think I was poisoned or drugged or something."

Ben, still shaken, mumbled beneath his breath, "If we're trying to figure out what draws people to this kind of music, it's clearly the dark side of things."

"Josh, would you like us to pray for you?" I asked, interrupting Ben.

"Really?" Josh laughed out loud. "Funny you would ask. Because I've been wondering tonight if I should experiment *more* with the powers of darkness. It seems to me all this God stuff is just a joke," he added, tears welling up in his eyes.

"Well, Josh, let's pray for you and see what happens," I answered.

"What the hell, right?" he croaked. "My night can't get any worse."

"Heavenly Father," Don spoke aloud while he and I placed our hands on Josh's head. "We pray that darkness would stay away from Josh and this current situation.

Please show Yourself to Josh and develop a loving relationship with him."

Ben and James prayed along with us.

"Lord," I added in quiet voice, "keep the forces of darkness away and keep them from deceiving Josh. We ask for healing in his spirit, mind, and body. And Lord, I pray specific healing for Josh's hand and powerful healing for any poison or drug that was giving to him. In Jesus' name, amen."

Suddenly Josh screamed and stumbled backwards. "What's going on? I feel heat all over my body. What did you all do to me?"

"Look at your hand!" Don cried out.

Josh's fist was glowing. Right in front of all our eyes, the swelling left like a popped balloon.

"The pain is gone!" Josh yelled as he jumped up and down. "I don't feel any more pain. My head has cleared. I don't feel drugged anymore. What just happened?"

We grinned at him.

"The swelling in my hand is gone," he said, still confused. He repeated his next question again and again. "What just happened? What just happened?"

"My friend," I responded, "Jesus just happened!"

You'd think that I would have been walking on clouds. And I was. For a season. But before long, darkness fell on me in a way I never would have imagined.

10

THE ROAR OF THE LION

"WHAT'S WRONG WITH ME, DON?" I asked, "We've seen God's power over and over, yet I am battling depression."

Six months had passed since our encounters with Throne Guy and Josh.

During those months, Don and I had both experienced losses, as several friends of ours had died from various circumstances. Chad lost his battle with brain cancer after years of fighting the disease. He and his wife attended our church and were friends of ours.

Bob, who was an elder at our church died from a heart attack a few weeks after Chad. Ed, who I became good friends with at my warehouse job, died in his sleep of a brain aneurysm. Heartache after heartache cracked my emotion's protective coating.

The final blow, our friend Geoffrey had committed suicide after years of chronic pain from a degenerating spine. And I was still processing the loss of Gwen, who had died before Don, and I traveled to New York for our summer of ministry.

"It's normal Rob, you're grieving," Don assured me. "We all are grieving the loss of our friends."

"But I'm really struggling," I confessed. "I feel like I am in a season of darkness."

Don was quiet a moment before admitting, "Me, too."

We both sat with that for a few minutes. Then Don added, "But how can we feel this way after all we've experienced? After last summer? All the powerful battles we watched God win against darkness?"

"I know. I feel so guilty." I said, blowing out a big sigh. "Things started changing after losing Geoffrey. That hit me hard."

After Geoffrey died as he did, I had nothing left. I stopped playing and singing on the streets of Boulder and Denver. I pulled myself away from the church I was attending. I stopped helping the poor. I needed to reexamine my beliefs. For the past ten years, I had been taught that God would answer any prayer, that vitality and prosperity were ours for the taking—like making a selection at a vending machine. And I had personally witnessed unbelievable answers to prayer. But seeing hardships that prayer didn't fix—like for Gwen and Geoffrey and others—made me question everything. Had I been on the wrong path all along? I was frightened of the answer. It's hard to passionately tell people that God loves them and wants to heal them when your friends and family are dying around you.

And what about me?

For months I wallowed in self-pity. I thought about all the time I had invested. I had been so focused on ministry, what could I have been doing with my life instead? What had I missed out on? Part of me felt that I had been sitting on the side lines of life while watching my friends graduate from college, get married, start families. I'd been singing on street corners year after year. Was it worth it? I asked myself repeatedly.

But on other days, I remembered all the amazing demonstrations of God's supernatural power in my life, starting when he healed my eyes when I was in first grade. Not to mention everything He had shown me since: Healing my grandmother. Protecting me in the city. Tearing down strongholds of darkness. Healing Josh.

How in the world could I be having a crisis of faith? And why does this dread of letting everyone down keep sneaking in? I asked myself these questions repeatedly, repentantly. I thought of the verse, "If I speak in the tongues of men or of angels, but do not have love, I am only a resounding gong or a clanging cymbal" (1 Corinthians 13:1). Had I turned into a resounding gong and a clanging cymbal? My guilt was excruciating! It haunted me.

"The pain wore him down," Don reminded me. "There was no relief in sight."

"But at church he always had such a beaming smile and engulfed people in big hugs," I said, remembering our friend. "I can't believe he's gone."

"His wife told me something about him was different that day," Don whispered. "The day he took his life."

"Why didn't God answer our prayers Don?" I asked,

adding, "I'm tired." I slumped back on the couch and confessed, "It's not helping that I am spending less and less time in prayer."

"We live in a sin filled world. Sin allowed death into the world."

"I know. I know that death will be the last enemy that Jesus defeats. But to be honest, my struggles began months before Geoffrey killed himself."

"Where's that Scripture about the foxes of doubt nibbling away at the roots of our beliefs?" Don asked.

"I think it's in the Old Testament," I answered. "I keep thinking of the verse about the lion's roar putting fear into its prey."

"Fear is a powerful force," Don agreed.

"I am afraid," I said. "Afraid I'm letting God down."

11

I WANT TO BELIEVE

"I WANT to believe our pastors have good intentions," I said, talking on the phone with Jena, a friend from church. "But I'm not sure everything we've been taught is true."

"But some things are true, right? A lot of things," Jena said, trying to get me out of my funk. "Like how to pray for people in a more personal way. Or how to read and study the Bible to build our faith."

"I know." I sighed. "And how important it is to have people praying for us. And the importance of fasting. And serving others."

I fell silent, reflecting on my own words.

"Hello? You still there?" Jena asked, breaking the awkward lull in the conversation.

"Sorry. I am just struggling in my mind, conflicted between my suspicions of the church and my gratefulness for the things I've learned from them."

"You're not alone. There are a few of us who feel the same way."

"I'm exhausted!" I blurted out. "I'll talk to you tomorrow and thanks for calling. And, Jena, don't worry. I'll work through this."

"Ok Rob, I'll talk with you soon. Keep the faith."

After Jena hung up, I thought, *Easier said than done. I hope I can get through this.* Knowing that people were praying for me gave me hope.

In the meantime, people who didn't know I was struggling continued to ask me to pray for them. Sometimes I was approached by people I barely knew. Occasionally even coworkers asked if I would say prayers before company sponsored lunches. As I obliged these prayer requests, I reminded myself that God will never leave or forsake me. And praying for others kept a faint light glowing inside me.

When family and friends asked me to pray for their healing, I did my best with the little faith I had. Some people were healed, and some were not. But God's comfort always showed up. I felt humbled every single time someone expressed their gratefulness for my prayers. It encouraged me, and I continued to pray when asked. Seeing people receive hope made the light glow stronger inside me. Because I prayed more for others, I believe I also felt His mercy and grace move back into my life. As I prayed healing for myself, God mended me or led me to people to show me how to repair my afflictions. What a merciful God!

My lifeline? I forced myself to read and pray through the book of Psalms.

Psalms acted as my gyroscope in the midst of my storms. The words in Psalms gave me peace and guidance and kept the strain of fearing my worth at bay. Sometimes, though, I read passages from the first four books of the New Testament. One day I came across a story Jesus told to his listeners. He said to him, 'If they do not listen to Moses and the Prophets, they will not be convinced even if someone rises from the dead.'" (Luke 16:31 NIV)

How could people experience Jesus, see His miracles, and eventually witness his resurrection and still doubt?

How could I?

I took a deep breath and shouted, "ENOUGH!"

I made my decision. "Lord," I said boldly each day, "I pray that you open my eyes to deception and rebuild my faith on solid ground. Help me strip away any teachings that are not from you."

Over time, I mentally created a slate of my beliefs and wiped it clean. I wiped away things I had believed that weren't supported in Scripture or life: beliefs that we never have to be sick or die, as well as the prosperity message of demanding that God give us whatever we want.

One by one I erased many of the doctrines I had been taught.

One day I prayed, *Lord, I'm emotionally raw. There's nothing left to believe in.*

"What about Jesus the King of kings?" God asked. "Will you still believe in Me?"

Was I hearing Him audibly? In my mind? I'm not sure. Questions raced through my mind.

Can I completely turn my back on my core convictions?

Can I turn my back on my relationship with God that I have leaned on since the first grade?

Can I turn my back on my friend, Savior and Lord, Yeshua Hamashiach (the Anointed One)?

Can I turn my back on what Jesus did on the cross?

Can I turn my back on His resurrection?

All these questions created stabbing pains in my heart.

"Lord I ask for light to dispel the darkness in me," I whispered.

Instantly, He filled my mind with two Bible verses:

> We are a most wretched people if we believe that Christ did not rise from the dead. (I Corinthians 15:17)

> If you confess Jesus is Lord and believe in your heart that God raised Him from the dead, you will not perish but have eternal life. (Romans 10:9)

My pulse slowed down, and my mind stopped racing. The piercing pain in my heart subsided. Stillness blanketed me, and joyfulness filled my soul.

I know!

I know that I know that God gave Himself. He sent His only Son who died for us, taking our punishment for sin.

I know that I know that Jesus conquered death and rose

from the dead and will return to set things right and dispel evil once and for all.

This is unshakable for me.

I heard a response in my spirit: "Not a belief but friendship."

Thinking of everything He has done for us—for me—I was overcome with emotion. With newfound confidence and strength, I proclaimed: "This is my foundation. This is my core belief. This is me. I can't turn my back on Him. Mercifully, I run toward Him." Yes, even with my doubts, anger, questions, and shortcomings.

Although I was joyful, the process was painful and gut-wrenching. I remained emotionally raw for a long time. But being at peace with my decision, I asked God to help rebuild my life.

The Lord proceeded to put me back together. Within my heart, He began to grow different desires. He began to inspire me to create some of the things I thought I had missed out on during the past ten years.

Over time, I finished my college degree and received a master's degree. I started dating and eventual married the love of my life. I developed a new confidence which helped me excel in my job with a Fortune 5000 company. More opportunities presented themselves, which brought more success into my life. Rebuilding my spirit was a long arduous process.

I am so grateful that I stumbled across a traditional church at St. Francis Cabrini. Members welcomed me and met me where I was at emotionally and spiritually. Their contemporary music-filled teen services kept me recharged and spiritually mindful.

But the roar of the lion was incessant. As I set my intention to allow God to rebuild my body, mind, and spirit, the Accuser continued whispering to me:

You yelled at your employee in frustration! What kind of example is that?

You waved your fist and screamed and yelled at that driver who cut you off! How can you call yourself a Christian?

You're always angry and afraid. Don't you trust God?

You're a doubter. You're a failure, you're not really a Christian!

You let everyone down including yourself.

The devil knew all the fear-buttons to push. He knew my doubts about past teachings I had followed. He amplified my dread of not being good enough, not spiritual enough, not godly enough, not holy enough, not having enough faith. He poked at my insecurities about failing God.

Fear in all its forms allows Satan's lies to beat us up, causing us to be completely ineffective.

I continued to resist the Accuser's onslaughts by praying the words of Psalms and bathing myself in praise and worship at church. I meditated on Scripture, especially Romans 8:1, which gave some relief against my fears: "Therefore, there is now no condemnation for those who are in Christ Jesus" (Romans 8:1).

No condemnation!

12

THE CAMPING TRIP LIKE NO OTHER

SEVERAL WEEKS LATER, Al and Pat, two of my closest friends from my former church, called to check in on me. We hadn't seen each other in a while so, after some catching up, we decided to take a few days and go on a fishing and camping adventure.

"Wow! We're sure getting eaten alive by mosquitoes!" Pat lamented as he swatted the bugs away.

"Yeah, what gives?" I grumbled. "I thought Colorado didn't have mosquitoes."

It was crazy. Clouds of mosquitoes sporadically appeared while we hiked the three-mile horse trail leading to the camping area by the lake. With no way around these swarms, we had to walk through them. We doused ourselves with bug spray but not before I received mosquito bites up and down my arms. But go figure! My friends did not get any bites at all.

We scouted out a gorgeous camping spot looking over the lake.

It took the rest of the afternoon to set up camp. We each had a two-man tent, some supplies, and of course our fishing gear.

"Guys, I found the fire pit!" Al yelled. "For cooking all the fish we're gonna catch!"

We grabbed our fishing poles and headed down to the lake.

"Hey, I just felt a tug," Pat said, euphoric as he pulled in a fish. He landed a beautiful lake trout.

"I just got a hit, too!" Al shouted, feeling a tug and laughing with excitement. He reeled in a nice sized trout as well.

Pat cast again and in less than five minutes he got another hit. At the same moment, Al was reeling in another trout.

Me? Nothing.

I used the same tackle, the same bait, and casted practically in the same spot as Al and Pat.

But zilch. Not even a nibble.

I reeled in my line to check it, and everything looked fine. I cast out again into the same part of the lake but nothing. I tried a different part of the lake and changed the type of bait but nothing. Not one tug. It was frustrating—but kind of comical.

"It's getting dark," Al said, "let's call it a day"

"Don't worry, Rob," Pat laughed, "we'll share our bounty with you."

We packed up and headed back to camp.

"I'm amazed how the fish jumped on my hook," Pat said as he cleaned the fish.

"I've never had such easy pickings when fishing," Al

said, snickering at me.

"So why did I have such a hard time?" I asked. "The fish didn't come anywhere near my line."

"We noticed," Al said and both guys laughed hysterically at me.

"Hey, Rob," Al asked, flashing a big grin, "Do you suppose God is trying to get your attention?"

"Right," Pat chuckled. "First the mosquitos and then the fishing."

"Very funny," I answered while breading the fish. "Here, put these in the pan I'm starving."

As we were eating around the open fire, the conversation turned more serious.

"Rob," Pat said, "what's going on? You seem distant and depressed. And I haven't seen you around much."

"I am really questioning my faith and what we've been taught at church."

"Yeah," Al said, "I am doing the same thing. I am at peace with the basics. It's just the extreme stuff I am having a hard time believing."

"I know we were ribbing you, Rob, about the fish—but maybe there's something to it. Maybe that's why you didn't catch any fish and why you were bitten by mosquitos. To get your attention. Maybe God doesn't want you doubting," Pat warned.

"Maybe," I replied. "But I think doubt can also be good. It's good to questions things to make sure we are not being deceived."

"That makes sense," Al said.

"But you left the church," Pat added.

"It's an ongoing, painful process," I said. "But I had

to do something to break this darkness around me. I want to be confident and have a firm foundation of faith—but that's hard to do when I'm questioning a lot that the church has taught me."

"Like what?" Al asked.

"Well, like about healing. I know God heals. And does miracles. And overcomes evil. And blesses people financially. I've seen it happen too often to think otherwise. But sometimes people aren't healed. Sometimes people die. Sometimes evil wins. Sometimes there is hardship instead of prosperity. Is God not God in those times, too?"

"So how are you working through this?" Al asked.

"Right now, I am focused on what Jesus did for us on the cross. Slowly, I am rebuilding on Him, and we will see where it leads me."

I stood to collect the dishes to clean up. "I'm tired. I think I will turn in for the night."

"Sleep well."

"You, too."

The next day we hiked up the trail that led to a side of a glacier and another lake.

The day started out glorious. The sun was shining, and there wasn't a cloud in the sky. We made sure to take water, trail mix, and light windbreakers. It was a shorts and T-shirt type of day, and all of us looked forward to an incredible July summer day hike.

The hike was invigorating just as we anticipated. Slow and steady we made our way up the incline.

It took us about an hour to reach the glacier lake.

God's creative abilities were showcased in the crystal-clear blue water of the lake with the snowcapped Rocky Mountains as the backdrop. Between us and the lake, lush green meadows colored with splashes of pink, blue, and yellow flowers blanketed the grounds. Breathtaking!

"Rob, isn't this amazing?" Pat marveled. "God sure knows how to create beautiful things. "How can you look at all that and doubt His active presence in our lives?"

"It *is* incredible," I agreed. "I never said I was doubting God's existence or His amazing works and creation on this earth. I'm questioning some of the teachings that seem to go beyond what He has shown us in Scripture. Where does He say that we will never get sick or experience hardships? Our church seems to teach that if you have enough faith, you don't even have to die!"

"Rob, none of us are sinless," Pat explained. "It's the sin in our lives and the world that allows sickness and troubles to enter our space. But it's not God's will for us."

"I think I agree with Rob on this one," Al mused. "I think these teachings present us with unattainable goals and when we fail, it crushes us and crushes our faith."

"Exactly!" I paused. "Don't get me wrong, God has spoiled me my entire life. He has healed me, protected me, and guided me through some tough times. But these teachings need to be questioned. I don't believe anymore that all of our hardships are because of our sin or lack of faith."

We were so involved in our theological discussions we didn't notice two hikers who had walked up on us.

13

THE CAMPING TRIP STRANGERS

"HELLO, my name is Skid, and this is Mark. Interesting conversation."

Startled by their sudden presence, we just sat there and stared.

"Sorry," he chuckled. "Didn't mean to eavesdrop. You just were all talking pretty loudly."

I laughed nervously. "I guess we were pretty intense—"

"You want my opinion?"

We didn't, but apparently he was going to give it to us anyway.

"Maybe the three of you should throw away your faith in this God and leave it in the trash where it belongs."

"Excuse me?" Al said in disbelief.

"Mark here," he said nodding toward his friend, "used to believe in God. Some TV preacher promised Mark that God would take all his problems away. But God didn't heal Mark from hepatitis. Did he, Mark?"

Mark shook his head.

"Lucky for Mark, he ran into me at a concert. I told him about the *real* supernatural forces that exist on earth in the here and now."

"Are you done?" Al said angrily.

"Darkness has yet to disappoint Mark," Skid bragged. "Right, Mark?"

Mark smiled a goofy grin and gave a slow nod.

"That's interesting," Pat said. "But I have yet to hear what Mark has to say about his so-called new life."

Skid answered, "He's a little wasted on psychedelic mushrooms right now. He's been throwing up for the last twenty-four hours, but he is having a great time. Nothing a little Jack Daniels won't fix."

"Did you just hear yourself?" Al asked with a disgusted look. "Mark is throwing up but having a great time!"

"I hate to tell you this, Skid, but what *you* are following belongs in the trash. You guys are being deceived and are being led straight to hell," Pat said with authority.

"What did you just say?" Skid asked through clenched teeth.

"Listen, Satan is a fallen angel who wants to destroy as many human lives as possible. He is doing this to get back at God for banishing him from heaven. He is destroying you; he is not giving you a dream life," Pat responded passionately. "He's the enemy and the only way to defeat this prince of the fallen angels is with faith in Jesus Christ and being cleansed by Jesus' blood." By the time Pat finished he was practically yelling at Mark and Skid.

When the words "Jesus' blood" came out of Pat's mouth both Skid and Mark recoiled like they were being burned by fire.

"Your faith doesn't help anybody. You can shove your fairy tales," Skid said. He then cursed at us, and they both turned and left as fast as they came upon us. "You just wait. Evil's gonna pay you a visit!" he called out as they departed.

We were all a little shaken by the encounter and discussion of the underworld.

"Can you believe those guys!" Al exclaimed. "They really seemed to believe what they were telling us. Throwing up and having a grand old time. It's incredibly sad."

"Well," I said, "it sort of proves my point about some of our teachings. They set up people for failure and then it hurls them into a crisis of faith. I've been there and done that." I took a deep breath and said, "Thank God, He never leaves us nor forsakes us. I really do appreciate His hand always being there for me."

"Amen," Al said before glancing at his watch. "Wow! It's four o'clock, it's time for us to head back to camp."

We all agreed.

It was late but not that late. The temperature was still a warm eighty degrees, and a wonderfully refreshing mountain breeze was coming in from the west, making the beginning of our hike back to camp very comfortable. We had about a one- or two-hour hike back with steep switch backs to navigate. The trail didn't seem as rocky coming up as it was going down. We had to watch our footing because of all the loose, small rocks coming off the trail. I hit a patch of pebbles, and it was just like hitting a patch of ice.

"Dang nab it" I exclaimed as my feet came out from under me and ouch, I landed on my butt.

"Watch out below," Al yelled as he came sliding down the path.

"Darn I think I scraped my hand," Pat shrieked as he slid down in front of me.

When we all came to a stop, we were a jumbled mess, twisted and somewhat shocked at the difficulty of the hike back down.

I looked at Pat. Al looked at me, and we all broke out laughing uncontrollably. I laughed so hard that my side started to ache. We helped each other up, being careful not to slip again, and brushed ourselves off.

"I don't remember this path being so gravelly," I said.

"Me neither," Al exclaimed.

"Hey, do you guys feel the temperature dropping?" I asked, feeling a chill in the air.

"Wow! Look at the sky. It's getting pitch black." Al sounded worried.

"That's weird, there aren't any storm clouds," Pat said looking up. "As a matter of fact, there's not a cloud in the sky."

"It's odd how this dark sky came upon us so quickly," Al wondered aloud.

"I don't know about you guys, but I am freezing.

How can this be? It was eighty degrees five minutes ago," I said blowing into my hands to warm them up.

"I'm freezing too," Pat said while warming his hands too. "It doesn't make sense for this time of year, especially when five minutes ago it was so warm."

"Hey guys remember what those guys said before they left us?" I asked.

"I was thinking the same thing," Pat blurted out.

"Let's pray," Al said.

"We rebuke any attack from the evil one and ask the Holy Spirit to protect us and get us back to camp safely. Amen," Al prayed.

"Amen," Pat and I said in agreement.

It felt like the temperature had dropped another ten degrees. We were freezing and having a hard time seeing because of the blanket of darkness that engulfed us.

"Hey guys I am afraid something terrible is going to happen. My balance feels off," I cried out.

"It looks like a treacherous part of the trail coming up ahead," Pat yelled. "I don't remember that steep, sharp drop-off on the side of the path. Did we make a wrong turn?"

"I can't tell," Al answered.

"We're quickly approaching that drop-off guys" I warned. Nervous I started to sing worship songs.

"I rebuke and chase away any evil spirits that might be here to hurt us," Al prayed loudly.

"Keep us safe, Lord," Pat yelled.

Slowly we hiked toward the cliff. The temperature was still dropping. We didn't bring flashlights and the blackness was setting in all around. It was treacherous to be hiking in the dark.

"Stop!" I yelled. "We are not going to make it past the drop-off. We can't see, and we are stumbling around like drunkards."

Let's pray for guidance from the Lord," Pat suggested.

We stopped again and fell silent.

Standing in the dark stillness we prayed calmly to ourselves.

No rumblings of thunder, no rain or wind, just an eerie darkness, and bone-chilling coldness.

"Hey Al, hey Pat, let's agree together again and ask God to warm us up and dissipate the darkness, so we can get home safely," I suggested.

Before we finished praying, I felt a nudge in my gut (spirit) to start heading down the path.

"I feel we need to start walking down the path," Pat said.

"We need to head down the path now," Al commanded.

His still, quite voice moved all three of us to hike down the dangerous path in faith and not to stay put because of fear. But I must admit fear kept trying to attach itself to all three of us.

Slowly we descended on the path toward the treacherous cliff. I stumbled and fell but got right back up. The path narrowed to a little more than a couple of feet between us and the cliff. The wind started to howl just as Pat's foot slipped off the side. Al and I rushed to him, stopping his momentum just in time. He was shaken up but got right back up on his feet and pushed on.

"Do you feel that?" I asked. "It's like a cocoon of warmth around me. Do you guys feel that? It's like being inside a heated bubble." No one answered. Feeling uneasy, I began singing songs of praise. I was scared but encouraged by my newfound warmth.

For some reason, I looked up from my steely concentration on the path in front of me and saw orange slits in the darkness. Rays of sunshine were piercing through the charcoal sky.

"Hooray!" I shouted as we made it safely down the mountain path.

"Praise Jesus!" Pat yelled.

"Thank You, Lord," Al screamed for joy.

Looking at each other, we let out a collective sigh of relief.

Pat was still shaking from the cold, and Al and I had some bumps and scratches. But we made it relatively unscathed to the flat trail that led to our campsite.

"The feeling of being in a warm bubble kept me going," I told the guys on the way back to camp.

"I felt like I was on a hoverboard floating over the rocks," Pat said, excitedly describing what kept him going.

"I kept seeing a small spotlight on the path to light my way," Al said, thankful for what kept him going.

"Chalk one up to the Big Guy today," I exhaled.

"It's a miracle we made it down safely!" Pat said shaking his head.

"Okay let's figured out what we are going to do for dinner," Al said.

We had a great time roasting hot dogs, and we made some baked beans. They tasted oh so good.

"What a day!" Pat exclaimed after finishing his dinner. "Thanks, guys, for being there to keep me from falling off the cliff."

"Yea," I said jestingly, "if you slipped off the cliff it would have really ruined our day." Laughing, I continue, "You know with all the paperwork dealing with all the rescue crews and police and everything."

"Yea, Rob, we probably would have had to shorten our camping trip as well," Al teased.

Our laughter filled the silence of the night and brought soothing comfort to our bodies, minds, and spirits.

Thankful for God's intervention, I felt my inner light shining a little brighter.

14

MY DYING FRIEND JOE

DURING MY SPIRITUAL REBUILDING, I needed to hire a part-time delivery driver at the company I worked for, and a man named Joe answered my ad. If I remember correctly, he was the dad of one of my coworkers.

When Joe came in for an interview with me, he greeted me with a firm handshake.

"Hi, Joe, thanks for coming in," I said, motioning for him to sit down. Then I continued in my "all business" voice, "Assignments fluctuate and working hours change as well, but the weekly hours will never go over three days a week, five hours a day. Would that work for you?"

"That is just what I am looking for," Joe answered. Then he added, "I am currently in treatment for cancer, and I usually can't function more than three days per week. Actually, I was hoping for two days a week, but I think I can make this work" he said, looking nervously down at his feet.

"Well, Joe, as I explained, this is a pretty flexible position. I think we can work around your schedule. We can even look at doing shorter days if that would help."

As I was speaking, a passion to help this man welled up inside me. If I had to be more flexible with the position to meet Joe's needs while he was fighting his illness, that is what I would do.

Joe started working for me that week. He did things like delivering packages between buildings, distributing mail, and shredding documents.

Joe and I became friends. He had a great sense of humor and was very reliable. We ate lunch together and had insightful conversations about politics, religion, and everything in between. We always ended our time together laughing hysterically. Joe was a genuinely good guy.

I was working in my office early one morning when my phone rang. I picked up.

"Rob, here. How may I help you?"

"Hi, Rob, this is Joe." His voice sounded strained. "Sorry for the last-minute notice, but I didn't have a good night last night. I need to go see my doctor. I don't think I can make it in today. The way I am feeling, I'll probably be out tomorrow as well. I am deeply sorry. I will give you a call tomorrow and give you an update."

"No problem, Joe. I'll get one of the guys to cover for you. Just concentrate on getting better."

I hung up the phone slowly.

Joe never did come back to work. Just like that, one minute Joe and I were laughing and the next he became bedridden. His family arranged for home care so he could stay in familiar surroundings. Later that week, I called Joe's daughter to ask how he was doing.

"Not very well," she said, sounding distraught. "The doctors are not giving him much time. They said he maybe has weeks left and is on hospice."

"Dee, if you can think of anything I can do—"

"I know, Rob. I'll let you know, I promise."

Early the next morning my office phone rang.

"Hi Rob, this is Dee. I told Joe you were asking about him, and he wanted me to ask if you would visit him sometime and pray with him."

"Yes, of course," I answered without hesitation. "When?"

"How about tomorrow after you finish up at work?"

"That would be perfect. Where?" I jotted down the address she gave me.

We said our goodbyes, and I hung up the phone.

Oh man what have I agreed to? I immediately thought to myself. I didn't mind agreeing to visit Joe, but praying for him to get better stressed me out. "Do I really still believe in healing?" I asked out loud.

I wasn't sure.

"Ok," I said, still talking to myself aloud. "What do I usually do when I'm facing a stressful situation? Prayer!" I yelled, hitting myself on the side of the head. "I turn to prayer with Jesus."

For me, prayer has never been pompous or ritualistic. I don't need to go to a church or any special place. I just start the conversation in my head.

"Lord, how can I pray for Joe?" I whispered. "I feel so unworthy because of all my questions and unbelief that I can barely pray for myself. I guess I could give Joe as much support and comfort as I can and not offer to pray for healing."

"Who is responsible for doing the miracles and healing?" I heard (or felt or thought—I really can't explain it) Him asking me. "You or Me?"

"Well, definitely You, God," I answered.

"Correct. So why are you putting all this pressure on yourself to perform a perfect healing prayer? Do you presume to think you know the mind of God? Rob, you know I can heal. You have seen and experienced it firsthand. Go to Joe, pray with him to receive my comfort, and let Me do the rest."

I felt the weight of the world lift from my shoulders.

"Wow!" I exclaimed loudly. "I have no power to heal—but I can be a comfort to others in difficult times. I can be a force for good without being perfect."

I spent the rest of the day praying for Joe's comfort and, if it was God's will, his healing.

The next morning, I felt nervous again. "Lord, help me channel my nervousness into prayer for Joe," I whispered. *After all, it's not like I am going to be graded.* I laughed at the thought.

For the rest of the day, I prayed for Joe. My workday ended on time. No last-minute emergencies for me to handle. I called Joe's house to make sure he was still up for my visit. His wife told me that Joe was somewhat unresponsive but would still love to see me. I left the office and went to my truck. I pulled out the directions to Joe's house and started the engine for the fifteen-minute drive.

Nervousness raised its head again. I was determined not to let it win. Singing praise songs at the top of my lungs, I thanked God for all the good things he had done in my life and for keeping me safe even when I ran away from Him. Singing always bolsters me, and I arrived at Joe's house filled with hope. Dee met me at the door. In fact, Joe's entire family was there, including both of his daughters, his wife, son-in-law, and a brother.

Oh no! I thought. I have to pray in front of all these people?

"Hi, I'm Joe's wife," a woman said, giving me a hug. "I've heard so much about you. Thank you for coming over."

She led me to a small area next to the laundry room where a hospital bed had been set up for Joe. His eyes were closed. I felt awkward, like I did not belong there. By then more visitors had arrived, and they were waiting in the living room for their turn to crowd into Joe's little room.

I held Joe's hand and whispered, "Hi Joe, it's Rob."

He opened his eyes and gave me a smile.

"He isn't speaking much today," his wife said to me.

We just sat there for a while, Joe, and I, holding hands in silence. I felt Joe squeeze my hand and try to pull me toward him. I leaned over.

"Rob," he whispered. "I am afraid. I know I am dying, and I am afraid of death. I have gone to church all my life and tried doing good." His breath was labored. "But lately I have had some time to think about things and about our conversations about Jesus."

He tried to sit up but fell back in the bed.

"Do you believe in Jesus and believe He's your Savior?" I quietly asked in his ear.

"Yes, I do believe. Rob, would you pray for me?"

"I would be honored to pray for you." While still holding Joe's hand, I placed my other hand on Joe's head.

"Father, I ask for forgiveness for all my sin and claim the precious blood of Jesus over my spirit, mind and body. I come to You humbly and ask that you give Joe comfort in his time of need. I ask by the power of the Holy Spirit that you bring healing to Joe's body, mind, and spirit. We praise You that Joe has confessed You as Lord and believes You raised Jesus from the dead. We thank you that he is saved."

I paused and noticed a small crowd forming outside of Joe's room. I could hear their whispers of prayer and comfort for Joe. I felt a warm light fill Joe's room as the small crowd of people broke into praises to God.

In silence Joe and I allowed the worship and praising of God wash over us.

"We thank you Father," I added, "that you hear our prayers and continue to give Joe Your healing, comfort, and joy. I pray in Jesus' name, amen."

Tears flowed out of Joe's eyes and mine. Everyone around us was crying, too.

"Thank you," Joe mouthed as he motioned me to put my ear close to his mouth. "Rob, I am no longer afraid," he whispered.

I hugged him and said my goodbyes to Joe and his family and let myself out. I praised God all the way home knowing it was now in His hands.

Dee called me the next day to tell me that Joe passed

away during the night. She said he died peacefully and had songs of praises to God on his lips.

I thanked her for letting me know, hung up the phone, and wept for the passing of my friend.

I marveled at the goodness of God.

Joe was no longer afraid. And neither am I!

EPILOGUE

EARLIER IN MY FAITH WALK, I felt like I had all the answers. If I had enough faith—and kept sin out of my life—God would give me exactly what I was praying for. I was calling the shots. That was a lot of pressure to live under, and a lot of presumption on my part. And when people in my life died, it gave Satan the ammunition to attack my faith.

When we see God's answers to our prayers as a litmus test of whether we are good or spiritual enough, it's no wonder we are afraid to pray. We don't always know what God wants to do, or how he wants to answer our prayers. When we see God's answers to our prayers as something that's totally up to Him, it's incredibly freeing. That means if He chooses not to heal someone, I can trust Him with that. And that means I don't need to be afraid to ask Him for miracles or healing.

Joel Osteen once told a story about a man who asked

him, "What if I keep believing God for healing, but I don't get healed?"

Joel answered, "Well, what if you keep believing God for healing and you *do* get healed?"

Prayer isn't a formula.

It's a relationship.

I like to think that with getting older I've become somewhat wiser. I now live a more balanced and quiet life. I no longer feel the need to charge into the dangers of the lion's den. My desire to engage in confrontations with people who have different beliefs than me has dwindled. If someone asks me about my beliefs, I gently tell of my faith in Jesus and what He has done for me and humanity—and most importantly how He has an unconditional love for everyone.

I pray for the people God brings into my life, asking God to guide, comfort, and lead them to Himself, to give them inner peace. I pray daily that God keeps me, my family and everyone I come in contact, from evil and keeps us from being deceived in this tricky world. I pray He allows us to enter a deeper relationship with Him and experience daily, His all-encompassing love.

I continue to believe that God heals, preforms miracles, and meets our needs according to His riches and glory. But I submit to the fact that He is calling the shots. He is my hope. God directs, comforts, and protects me—but in His way and in His timing.

Most important, I'm not afraid anymore. When bad things happen—even death—it doesn't undermine my faith. Because my faith isn't in the results, but the person of Jesus.

EPILOGUE

I know it seems obvious, yet it has taken me some time and soul searching to accept the idea that death is part of life. Dying is the last battle we face here on earth. And in faith, it is our final winning blow against evil. With Jesus, when it's our time, we never have to die alone.

It's hard to ignore the fact that people are hurting and looking for answers. Most are looking for something, anything, to fill the void of their lost faith, grief, disappoints, and hopelessness.

I listen with a heavy heart as people call to the universe, the stars, or idols for comfort. Maybe they get relief, but it will be fleeting at best. In the book of Psalms it says, "They multiply their sorrows who court other gods" (Psalm 16:4 NABRE). And yet it's the Creator of the universe who will fill their void and give them the comfort they so desperately need. For that reason, I strive to let my light shine as Mother Teresa suggests: "Let no one ever come to you without leaving better and happier. Be the living expression of God's kindness: kindness in your face, kindness in your eyes, kindness in your smile."

Wherever God has you today, give hope to those around you. Your purpose is to minister wherever God places you, whether that's preaching on a street corner, raising a family, running a company, or being nice to a stranger.

I suspect I fail at living this way more than I succeed, but I stay positive and persevere. And wherever God calls me in each season of my life, I ask Him to help me forget yesterday's failures, live gratefully for today's blessings, and trust Him with tomorrow.

Does God exist? Yes, and He is reaching out to all of us through Jesus Christ.

Does Satan exist? Yes, and he wants to destroy as many lives as possible.

But Jesus said, "I have told you these things, so that in me you may have peace. In this world you will have trouble. But take heart! I have overcome the world" (John 16:33).

ABOUT THE AUTHOR

Rob Filogomo has done many things over the course of his life. Starting off as a four-year-old vibraphonist, he performed on TV on *The Sunny Fox Show*. He went on to play in coffeehouses; church groups; and on the streets of Colorado, New York, and Paris.

Tiring from the hard life of a musician, Rob switched gears, went back to school, and received his master of science in information systems. He has managed data centers, dental offices, and a non-profit before retiring in Sun City, Arizona.

During his retirement he has taught himself video editing, photography, and building websites, primarily to support his wife's blog.

Rob is Sicilian and loves food. Life to him is enjoying a spectacularly prepared meal with special friends. He and his wife have fun exploring new, interesting restaurants, museums, and other events such as a guided scorpion night hike in the White Tank Mountains.

Visit: www.robfilogomo.com or www.filofeast.com

www.ingramcontent.com/pod-product-compliance
Lightning Source LLC
Chambersburg PA
CBHW021446070526
44577CB00002B/285